W9-ARQ-450

Mark Twain's
THE ADVENTURES OF HUCKLEBERRY FINN

AND OTHER WORKS

ALEXANDER J. BUTRYM
DEPARTMENT OF ENGLISH
SETON HALL UNIVERSITY

MONARCH PRESS

Copyright © 1964 by
SIMON & SCHUSTER, Inc.

All rights reserved. No part of this book may be re-
produced in any form without permission in writing
from the publisher.

Published by
MONARCH PRESS
a division of Simon & Schuster, Inc.
1 West 39th Street
New York, N.Y. 10018

Standard Book Number: 671-00649-5

Library of Congress Catalog Card Number: 65-7243

Printed in the United States of America

CONTENTS

A BIOGRAPHICAL SKETCH OF MARK TWAIN

In order to make anything out of himself, Mark Twain had to struggle pretty hard with an environment that was against him from the beginning. Born Samuel Langhorne Clemens in the one-horse village of Florida, Missouri, in 1835, he rose to become a world famous writer, lecturer and traveler before he died in 1910. Most of his success was due to a combination of indomitable drive, unceasing energy, maximum use of his own talent, and some luck.

BASIC FACTS: The basic facts of Twain's life are well known. Four years after he was born, the family moved to Hannibal, Missouri, a village just a little larger than his birthplace. During his boyhood he had all the advantages and disadvantages of growing up in a country environment. He was close to the big river, and probably spent time exploring its wooded shores and islands. He grew up in tune with the life around him, swimming and playing hooky from school, and falling in love and reading (for his family was an intelligent one). Upon his father's death in 1847, Sam Clemens became a printer's apprentice. He followed his trade over a good part of the country, working in towns as different as Keokuk and New York. But the pay wasn't too good for printers in those days, so after trying unsuccessfully to get to South America, he became a river pilot. What had happened was that he thought he would go to South America to make some easy money. Before he got to New Orleans to take ship, however, he became friendly with a river pilot named Horace Bixby, who promised to teach him the river. Bixby was a good pilot, one who loved his work and established a reputation for excellence. The story of Twain's apprenticeship is told in *Life on the Mississippi*. The account is "stretched" somewhat, as Huck Finn would say.

After piloting the steamers for about four years, Clemens retired to the Nevada gold country, because the onset of the Civil War had put an end to river commerce. He eventually ended up in California, back at the printing trade. He wrote short pieces for the newspapers he worked on, establishing a reputation as a humorist among the provincial readers of the Old West. The result of this writing and some lecturing was that he fell in with a group of writers who have come to be known as the "Local Colorists." Men like Bret Harte and Artemus Ward—not much heard of today—were extremely popular in the West for tales which were woven from folk stories and written in dialect with rough-hewn humor and plenty of recognizable concrete detail.

SUCCESS AND MARRIAGE: In 1869 he published *The Innocents Abroad*, an account of a trip to Europe he made under the sponsorship of a newspaper. In the book, he satirizes the folly of going across the Atlantic to see dead men's graves when there are many more living things to see right here. The book made him famous, and gave him a literary reputation in the East.

As a successful writer he attained respectability enough to marry into a wealthy Buffalo, New York family. His wife's name was Olivia Langdon, of the socially prominent Langdons. Five years later he moved to Elmira, N.Y., and then to Hartford, Connecticut, where he had a house built. Most of this time was taken up with writing, for he had made friends with a number of interesting literary people, among them William Dean Howells, the famous author (*The Rise of Silas Lapham*) and editor (*The Atlantic Monthly*). During this period he wrote *Roughing It* and *The Gilded Age*. The former is a memoir of the early days in the West; the latter, written in collaboration with Charles Dudley Warner, another friend, is a satire on the way the federal government was run. In 1875 he began work on his first novel: *Tom Sawyer*. The book was a success.

HUCK FINN: In 1876 he sat down to its sequel, *The Adventures of Huckleberry Finn*. Although this is the work on which the greatest proportion of his literary fame rests, it was not an easy book to write. The history of its composition has been traced by Walter Blair, and is discussed in the *Introduction to Huck Finn*, below. It is sufficient to note here that the book didn't appear until 1884 in England, and 1885 in America. It was an immediate success, despite adverse criticism by some of the more conservative literary judges of the day.

Between 1876 and 1885 Twain had written several books, among them *The Prince and the Pauper, A Tramp Abroad, and Life on the Mississippi.* After Huck Finn, his next major work was *Pudd'nhead Wilson* (1889). Then came *A Connecticut Yankee in King Arthur's Court* (1894).

SORROWS AND DIFFICULTIES: Mark Twain's final years were not full of the satisfactions a man hopes to find at the end of a life well led. Instead he suffered a series of financial disasters and personal losses which would have taken the heart out of a lesser man. His publishing company failed in 1894, and shortly thereafter he lost a great deal of money which he had invested in a project to invent a typesetting machine. In spite of his advanced years—he was in his sixties—he took on a foreign lecture tour to pay back every cent he owed. By 1898 he was out of debt. But before he finished the tour, there began for him a series of losses which were to color the rest of his life. These were deeper losses, more personal than merely financial misfortunes. First, his daughter Suzy died, then his wife died, then his daughter Clara went with her husband to live in Europe. This left Clemens with only his daughter Jean, whose epilepsy resulted in a heart attack from which she died.

Four months after Jean's death, on April 21, 1910, Mark Twain died of a heart attack.

Disillusioned by business reversals and personal losses, he was a bitter writer toward the end of his days. Some of his later writings are just being published. They have been withheld from the public by his estate because of the savage nature of their biting satire.

His writings, from the earliest to those just appearing, can best be described as "iconoclastic." That is, they are "image breakers." The picture that most often comes to mind while one is reading his works is that of a man sitting on a hill overlooking a valley populated by foolish people. Every once in a while he shakes his head sadly at their folly and throws stones at the false symbols and standards they have raised. A terrible enemy to injustice and confusion, Mark Twain wrote scores of attacks on the villainous and fraudulent pursuits of dishonest people, and on the weak, insipid facades of hypocrisy.

AN INTRODUCTION TO THE ADVENTURES
OF HUCKLEBERRY FINN

HUCK FINN AND THE PICARESQUE: The story of Huck Finn's adventurous journey down the Mississippi River on a raft is really a series of short adventures. This is the kind of plot that is known in literature as an episodic plot. Each event is an episode, a self-contained little story. Plots like this are characteristic of a certain kind of novel, the picaresque novel. (This type of novel had its beginning in Spain during the sixteenth century. Among the first of these novels is one called *Lazarillo de Tormes.*) To say that *Huckleberry Finn* is a picaresque novel is incorrect, however, because there is something missing from it that would be necessary in a picaresque novel. In addition to having an episodic plot, picaresque novels have as their chief characters the low-life and criminal classes of a nation. While it is true that Huck Finn is not of the upper or even the middle class, he is not a proper picaresque hero because he is not hard-hearted and cruel and selfish enough. Perhaps Huck's pap might be a picaresque hero; certainly the king and the duke would be. But not Huck.

There is no doubt that Mark Twain borrowed from the traditions of the picaresque novel, particularly from *Don Quixote,* the novel by Cervantes that sprang from the picaresque tradition. But as with any literary genius, Mark Twain changed and shaped what he borrowed until it was something a little different, and good in its own way.

The story was begun by Mark Twain in 1876, but not completed until 1884 when it was published in England. The history of its composition has been told by Walter Blair in his book, *Mark Twain and Huck Finn.* When Twain got as far as Chapter 16, he ran into trouble. First, he didn't know what to do with the plot; it had gotten out of hand. There was no way to get Jim and Huck upstream once the raft and canoe are lost, and they are past Cairo. He had been working so hard he lost his inspiration to continue the book.

SHIFTS OF VIEWPOINT: So he laid it aside for a while. But notice how the first sixteen chapters of the book deal with Jim's escape from slavery. Every time freedom is talked about, Jim's freedom is meant. After the sixteenth chapter, Jim recedes into the background. He disappears from the story altogether in the Grangerford chapters, coming in only to save Huck from the "civilization" of plantation feuds. After this, even though the two travelers have a canoe, they make no effort to go back north to Cairo. Once the king and the duke come aboard, Jim is of no importance to the story until he is sold off. Then, when Tom Sawyer makes his appearance, Jim is no more than a minstrel-show-Negro until he sacrifices his freedom, and is picked up as a human character again.

This shifting around would be a major flaw in the novel if Jim were the central figure, or if his escape from slavery were the central theme of the story. But neither of these is true. The central figure of the story is Huck Finn: the story is told to us from his point of view—in the first person. Huck sees and reports; sometimes he understands what he sees, and so he interprets it. Sometimes he doesn't understand, and this too is significant. The central theme of the story is the theme set by the first and last chapters: Huck's fight against getting "sivilised." The civilization he is running from is peopled by characters like the Widow, Miss Watson, Pap, Aunt Sally, and Tom Sawyer, although Tom attracts Huck in a way.

CONTRAST: The story is full of striking comparisons, many of which are pointed out in the sections of COMMENT following the summary of each chapter. Indeed, there are so many of these comparisons and contrasts that at times Mark Twain seems to be burlesquing his own story. The swearing in of Tom Sawyer's robber-gang, for instance, is a clear foreshadowing of the events that take place on the wrecked *Walter Scott*. Tom's love of adventure and Huck's search for adventure (in the *Walter Scott* episode) are obvious parallels (see the *Essay Questions and Answers*).

There is also an obvious contrast in the character of Tom Sawyer and that of Huck Finn. Tom's ambition is to become famous without counting the cost to himself or others. The adventure's the thing; the hurt and anguish of Aunt Sally, the pain and discomfort of Jim, these never occur to him. But Huck, involved in real adventures, is continually bothered by his conscience. All during the trip down river, he tries to answer the question whether he's doing right by the Widow's sister and by Jim, or not. The preoccupation with justice has him on the horns of a dilemma. Whatever he chooses to do, he's wrong. He's wronging Jim if he returns him to slavery; he's wronging Miss Watson if he helps Jim escape. Huck has no way of knowing what is right. He must follow the dictates of his feelings every step of the way. The only thing he can do is learn by experience. And he does.

HUCK AND JIM: He learns from Jim, who is in some ways a substitute father for him. He doesn't believe in Jim's superstition until the superstition proves itself true. Note how he scoffs at the snakeskin, until the snakeskin does its work. Huck rises to this level. By accepting Jim's superstitions Huck enters Jim's primitive world which, though crude, is much more sincere and honest than Miss Watson's world. Beyond it he cannot go. He won't pray because he has not experienced any benefits from prayer.

THE SECOND PART: In the second part of the story—the chapters dealing with the Grangerford feud and the adventures of the king and the duke—we are taken on a tour of the Mississippi River valley. We see the romantic ideas of Tom Sawyer in their practical applications.

The Grangerfords, with their senseless pride and basic crudity, are held up as examples of the real culture of the South. Huck describes them, their house and its decorations. These descriptions seem to us to be descriptions of ignorant and arrogant people. We understand this, and we laugh at the sentimentality of Emmeline's poetry and paintings; but Huck. who also sees all this, doesn't understand what it means, and he doesn't laugh at it. He thinks it's noble. And so do all the members of the Grangerford family, and all their neighbors.

The king and the duke are illustrations of Tom Sawyer's desire to "promote" things when it has taken hold of grown-ups. These two men choose their own comfort at the expense of those around them. They trade on the ignorance, pride, and laziness of the residents of the villages along the mighty river's shore. They do just what Tom does when he draws up a coat of arms for Jim, a coat of arms that he himself doesn't understand, let alone Jim. And Huck accepts Tom just the same way he accepts the king and the duke. He shrugs an intellectual shoulder and murmurs something about how you can't get Tom to explain a thing to you if he doesn't want to. Tom's ambition is to get famous; the frauds want to get rich.

THE THIRD PART: Finally, the third part of the novel brings us back to Tom Sawyer as the focus of the plot. (Huck is still the main character in the novel, however. He is reporting all that goes on; and even if he doesn't seem to understand it, he is involved in it and he colors what he reports by just being what he is.) But it is this part of the novel that ties up all that comes before it. We see Tom as he is, a romantic, a muddle-head, but bound to be a successful community leader. He has visions of grandeur; he is capable of stupidly leading an escaped slave into a Southern village and having all the slaves who are still bound hold a torchlight parade in honor of the escaped slave. The only logical outcome of such goings-on would be the hanging of most of the slaves in the village. And this is undoubtedly what would have happened if Tom had not caught the bullet that night at the Phelpses' farm.

THE IDEALIST: We also see Huck as he is, the opposite of Tom. He is a realist, and generally level-headed except when he goes off after Tom Sawyer's adventure, or when he follows Tom's lead. He is not civilizable. The end of the book makes this clear. He is where he was in the beginning: he left the Widow's house, and he will leave Aunt Sally's. Something in civilization appalls Huck Finn.

So far as the mechanics of composition are concerned, Mark Twain was considerably limited by the fact that Huck Finn is a living, breathing personality who shines through the pages of the book. Since Huck Finn tells the story himself, in the first person, Mark Twain had to put himself in the place of this thirteen-year-old son of the town drunkard. Twain had to see life as Huck saw it. He had to conceive a character who

could believably see life as Mark Twain saw it. But Huck is more than
Twain's mouthpiece. As a living character he is capable of shaping the
story. The very language Huck uses colors what he sees and how he
will pass it on to us. Very obvious is the fact that the humor of the
book often depends on Huck's language. However, it is through his use
of language that Twain creates character and sets down objective truth.
The very innocence of Huck is reflected through his credulous explan-
ation of what he sees—explanations couched in language characteristic
of primitive, basic society. Huck is capable of making Twain write something merely because it is the kind of thing Huck would do or say; and
he can force Twain to leave something out because Huck would not
do or say that kind of thing.

DIALECTS: So far as the dialects of the characters are concerned, we
can only remark that Mark Twain was a master at reproducing the
speech of his day. He doesn't need to indicate the speaker's name. The
dialect indicates him just as exactly as if he were named. Twain uses,
he says, "The Missouri negro dialect; the extremest form of the back-
woods South-Western dialect; the ordinary 'Pike-County' dialect; and
four modified varieties of this last." The careful and consistent attention
to details of speech is one of the many characteristics of this book which
make it worth serious and careful reading. Mark Twain drew his knowledge of these dialects from personal experience. And it is the concrete
and graphic products of experience in this story which make it so
appealing.

THE MAIN CHARACTERS

HUCKLEBERRY FINN: This is the central figure of the novel, the son of the town drunkard. He is essentially good-hearted, but he is looked down upon by the rest of the village. He dislikes civilized ways because they are personally restrictive and hard. He is generally ignorant of book-learning, but he has a sharply developed sensibility. He is imaginative and clever, and has a sharp eye for detail, though he doesn't always understand everything he sees, or its significance. This enables Mark Twain to make great use of the device of irony. Huck is essentially a realist. He knows only what he sees and experiences. He doesn't have a great deal of faith in things he reads or hears. He must experiment to find out what is true and what isn't. With his sharply observant personality he is able to believe Jim's superstition at some times, to scoff at it at others.

THE WIDOW DOUGLAS: The wife of the late Justice of the Peace of St. Petersburg—the village which provides the story's setting. Huck likes her because she's kind to him and feeds him when he's hungry. Her attempts to "civilize" him fail when Huck prefers to live in the woods with his father. He doesn't like to wear the shoes she buys him, and he doesn't like his food cooked the way hers is.

MISS WATSON: The Widow's maiden sister. She leads Huck to wish he were dead on several occasions by trying to teach him things. Her favorite subject is the Bible. She owns Jim and considers selling him down river. This causes Jim to run away. Filled with sorrow for driving Jim to this extreme, Miss Watson sets him free in her will.

TOM SAWYER: Huck's friend. A boy with a wild imagination who likes to play "games." He reads a lot, mainly romantic and sentimental novels about pirates and robbers and royalty. He seldom understands all he reads; this is obvious when he tries to translate his reading into action. He doesn't know what "ransoming" is: he supposes it to be a way of killing prisoners. He has a great deal of drive, and can get people to do things his way.

JIM: Miss Watson's slave, and the one really significant human character Huck meets in the novel. Though he is referred to as Miss Watson's "nigger," it is clear that the expression is used as a literary device—it is part of the Missouri dialect of the nineteenth century. Aside from Huck, Jim stands head and shoulders above all the characters in the book, in every respect. He is moral, realistic, and knowing in the ways of human nature. He appears at times as a substitute father for Huck, looking after him, and helping him, and teaching him about the world around him. The injustices perpetrated by the institution of slavery are given deep expression in his pathos.

PAP: Huck's father, the town-drunkard. He is in every respect the opposite of Jim. He is sadistic in his behavior toward his child. He is dirty, greedy, and dies violently because of his involvement with criminals. He is typical of the "white trash" of the day. Pap is an example of what Mark Twain thought the human race was: unreformable. A person is what he is, for good or bad, and nothing can change him.

JUDGE THATCHER: The guardian of Tom's and Huck's money. He is very wealthy, and the most respected man in the village. He becomes involved in a lawsuit to protect Huck from the cruelty of his father.

THE GRANGERFORD FAMILY: Southern aristocrats of the pre-Civil War South. They are portrayed as men who are jealous of their honor and cold-blooded in revenge. They are excellent horsemen and good fighters, and they respect their enemies as being the same. Their women are sentimental, but accustomed to hard living. Their taste runs to plaster of paris imitations of things and melancholy poetry. The general influence of Sir Walter Scott's romantic novels is clearly seen in the details of these people's daily lives.

THE KING AND THE DUKE: Two river tramps and con-men who pass themselves off to Huck and Jim as the lost Dauphin of France and the unfortunate Duke of Bridgewater (Bilgewater). To make their living off suckers they find in the small, dirty, ignorant Southern villages. Of the two men, the duke is less cruel and more imaginative than the king; though neither has any moral sensitivity worth mentioning. These men represent the starkly materialistic ideals of "the man who can sell himself" in their most logical extreme. Mark Twain holds them up as examples of the anti-social tendencies of the human race. Readers are usually happy when they come to the part of the story where these two get tarred and feathered and ridden out of town on a fence rail. Huck is more human about their suffering.

THE WILKS GIRLS: Nieces of Peter Wilks, a dead man. The king and the duke try unsuccessfully to rob the girls' inheritance. Mary Jane, the eldest, causes Huck to almost fall in love with her. He admires her spunk, or "sand." Susan is the middle sister, and Joanna, the "Hare-lip," is the youngest. Joanna questions Huck about his fictive life in England. His discomfort at being caught in a situation where he can't lie very easily is removed by Mary Jane and Susan who berate Joanna for upsetting the peace and quiet of their guest. The girls are innocent sheep, ready for snatching by the king and duke. Only Huck of the three "visitors from England" feels sorry for their plight.

THE PHELPSES: Tom Sawyer's uncle and aunt. They buy Jim from the king and the duke. Kind, gentle people who do right as their consciences dictate. Sally is going to adopt Huck, but he would rather go live among the Indians.

AUNT POLLY: The aunt with whom Tom lives. She is fairly well off, a member of the middle class. With a nephew like Tom, she is long-suffering.

SID: Tom Sawyer's half-brother. He doesn't figure in this story, except that Tom uses his name because the Phelps family thinks Huck is Tom.

HUCKLEBERRY FINN
CHAPTER 1.   I MEET MOSES AND THE BULRUSHERS

Mark Twain's HUCKLEBERRY FINN opens with the hero of the story (Huck Finn) introducing himself as one of the characters who figured in another book by Mark Twain, TOM SAWYER. Huck tells us that "Mr. Mark Twain" was more or less truthful in telling the story of TOM SAWYER. On occasion Twain "dressed up" the story, but by and large he told it accurately. After all, Huck says, everybody lies once in a while —except maybe Tom Sawyer's Aunt Polly, or the Widow Douglas (the woman who took Huck into her home in an attempt to raise him), or Tom's cousin Mary.

At any rate, Huck continues, at the end of the other book he and Tom are rich because they found a robber's cave in which there was loot amounting to $12,000. With this money set out at interest, each of the boys gets a dollar a day spending money, "more than a body could tell what to do with." Huck tells us he soon tired of living a respectable life with the widow, so "when I couldn't stand it no longer I lit out." He found his old hogshead (the large barrel he slept in during his free and easy days) and was content again. Content, that is, until Tom Sawyer talked him into going back to the widow's house in order to put up a respectable "front." Tom, you see, was starting a band of robbers (another of Tom Sawyer's games), and Huck could join if he had a good reputation.

Huck then tells us how he felt cramped up in the clothes he had to wear at the widow's house—he preferred his old rags, at least he didn't itch and sweat in them. When the widow tried to teach him Bible stories (particularly "Moses and the Bulrushers"), Huck was interested until he found out that Moses was dead. When he learned that, he says, "I didn't care no more about him, because I don't take no stock in dead people."

Things got rougher when Huck asked the widow to let him smoke his corncob pipe, and she said no because smoking was crude and dirty. What Huck couldn't understand was the fact that the widow took snuff, and because she did it herself thought that snuff taking was all right.

Huck got into trouble with the widow's old maid sister, Miss Watson, who came to live with the widow about this time. Miss Watson tried to teach Huck to spell, but Huck couldn't stand it. When Miss Watson told him about Hell, Huck said he wished he were there—just so he could go somewhere, he felt he needed a change. But Miss Watson didn't understand, so she lectured Huck about evil and good and Heaven. Huck comments, "Well, I couldn't see no advantage in going where she was going [that is, to Heaven], so I made up my mind I wouldn't try for it." And anyway, Huck was glad he wouldn't get to Heaven because Miss Watson didn't think Tom Sawyer would get there.

At the end of the evening, Miss Watson and the widow call the slaves in and say prayers. Then everybody goes to bed. Alone in his room, Huck begins to feel lonesome and scared. His fear grows on him as he listens to the sounds in the night and finds superstitious meanings in such noises as the hooting of an owl and the baying of a dog. When he flips a spider off his shoulder into the flame of a candle where it shrivels up, Huck becomes more downhearted than ever.

He lights up his pipe—no one will know because everyone is asleep—and settles down with the stillness of the night. Then he hears twigs snapping and a quiet "me-yow! me-yow!" out in the yard. His mood brightens. He answers the call, puts out the light, shinnies down to the ground, and finds Tom Sawyer waiting for him.

> **COMMENT:** This chapter gives us an idea of the kind of person Huck Finn is. For all practical purposes he is an orphan: his mother is dead, and his father is the village drunkard—a mean person whom we'll meet in the next few chapters. As a result of his background, Huck has grown into a free-wheeling sort of person who is happiest when he has fewest social responsibilities. He doesn't think about religion the way other people do, because he seems more interested in the comforts of the moment. Huck is essentially superstitious, but he isn't hypocritical or sneaky. He doesn't like to get people excited, especially if it would do no good. He wants mainly to be left to his own devices, to sleep in his hogshead, to wear his old rags, and to eat his food all mixed up (because "the juice kind of swaps around, and the things go better").

CHAPTER 2.   OUR GANG'S DARK OATH

Tom and Huck start making their way through the widow's backyard when Huck trips and makes a noise. Miss Watson's slave Jim, who is sitting in the kitchen doorway, hears the noise, but because the light is behind him he can't see Tom and Huck. He calls out into the darkness. Since he gets no answer, he decides to outwait whoever is in among the trees. He sits with his back against a tree, about halfway between the two boys. Huck notices that whenever he's in a situation like this, where it isn't smart to move around, he begins to itch. But just as he thinks he can't stand the itching (in eleven different places) any longer, Jim begins to snore.

The boys crawl away, but before they leave, Tom sneaks into the kitchen and takes three candles. He puts a nickel on the table to pay for them. Then he crawls back to where Jim is sleeping and puts Jim's hat on a branch above his head. Huck explains that because of this game of Tom's, Jim thinks he's been "witched." He tells the rest of the slaves that the nickel he found in the kitchen is a charm given him by the devil. As a result of this night's adventure, Jim becomes highly respected by his comrades who are as superstitious as he is. Jim "stretches" the truth even more by saying that witches rode him all over the world.

The boys go to a hill overlooking the village. Here they meet Joe Harper and Ben Rogers and two or three more of their friends. They take a skiff—a clumsy, flat-bottomed boat—and go two and a half miles downstream, where they land. Tom makes everybody swear secrecy; then he shows them a cave in the hillside. The boys crawl into it. After going about 200 yards, they find their way into a large room, "all damp and sweaty and cold. . . ."

Here Tom explains his plan for forming a robber gang. He says, "Now, we'll start this band of robbers and call it Tom Sawyer's Gang. Everybody that wants to join has got to take an oath, and write his name in blood." Tom reads the oath—a gruesome one—and everybody signs. One of the articles of the oath is that the family of any gang-member who tells the gang's secrets must be killed. This leaves Huck out; he hasn't any family— since his father hasn't been seen in the village in over a year, everybody thinks he's dead. Huck remembers Miss Watson. He offers to let the gang kill her if he tells any secrets. The gang accepts Huck's offer, and he is allowed to mark his sign (Huck can't write, remember) in blood on the oath.

The boys discuss gang policy for a while. They decide—rather, Tom Sawyer decides—that they are highwaymen, not burglars. The reason is that highwaymen have more "class." This is also the reason why they will always kill their victims—there's more "style" in a gang that kills the people it robs than in one that doesn't. After some talk about ransoming victims—talk that shows Tom's knowledge is from books he doesn't understand too well—the gang goes home because little Tommy Barnes got scared and wanted his mother and threatened to tell all the gang's secrets. Tom bribes Tommy Barnes with a nickel. The meeting then breaks up with the gang resolving to "meet next week, and rob somebody and kill some people."

COMMENT: In this chapter we are introduced to Tom Sawyer and Jim, Miss Watson's Negro slave. We note that Jim seems to be a stereotype of others of his race and station in the Southern States during the early nineteenth century. (Much more will be said about Jim later in the book.) Tom is interesting, though. He is a leader among the boys of the village, and he has high romantic ideas. He especially likes to play games on people, as Huck says. We see this in the trick Tom pulls on Jim by placing Jim's hat in the tree, and in the oath taken by the boys when they form the robber gang. There is no chance at all of the boys' killing anyone, or stealing anything of great value—not while one of them is still crying for his mommy, and getting bribed to keep the gang's secrets. By and large we see that Tom Sawyer is different from Huck Finn in that Tom plays at rebelling against society, whereas Huck, as we saw in the last chapter, really wants to "get out from under" civilization.

CHAPTER 3. WE AMBUSCADE THE A-RABS

The next morning Huck gets a "going over" from the widow's sister, Miss Watson, because his clothes are all dirty from climbing around the cave the night before. The widow herself doesn't scold; she cleans off the clothes. Huck resolves to behave on the widow's account. He tells us that he can't see any reason for "hooking up" to Miss Watson's kind of religion. Whenever he prays he doesn't get what he wants. And as for the widow's kind of religion, Huck doesn't think he'll be a credit to it, "seeing I was so ignorant, and so kind of low-down and ornery."

Although Huck's drunkard father hasn't been seen in some time, and although the rumors are that he died—drowned in the river 12 miles north of the village,—Huck is not so sure his father won't be coming back soon. He is unhappy at the idea of his father coming back, because his father beats him and mistreats him.

At any rate, Huck and Tom and the rest of the boys play robber for about a month, until finally Huck and most of the other boys quit. They "hadn't robbed nobody, hadn't killed any people, but only just pretended." Tom explains to Huck that the gang never gets loot because the travelers—particularly the last ones, the A-rab caravan—have magic rings and magic lamps which they use to call genies to their aid. Huck doesn't believe all this. All he knows is that the A-rab caravan turned out to be a group of Sunday School children on an outing. However, he takes a ring and an old whale oil lamp into the woods with him "and rubbed and rubbed till I sweat like an Injun . . . but it warn't no use, none of the genies come." Huck concludes that Tom Sawyer was lying. He says, "I reckoned he believed in the A-rabs and the elephants, but as for me I think different. It had all the marks of a Sunday school."

COMMENT: This chapter continues giving the background information we are getting of Huck Finn and the people he is involved with. Huck is no enemy of organized religion; he just can't understand how it will do him any good. Notice how neither Tom Sawyer's magic lamps nor Miss Watson's prayers give him any satisfaction. Huck prays for fishing gear, but only gets the line—which is useless without hooks. He rubs the lamp, calculating to have a genie build him a palace he can sell, but no genie comes. Notice also Huck's attitude of letting every man believe what he wants to. Huck doesn't tell Tom the truth about the Sunday school outing; he says instead "I think different." A similar thing happened in Chapter One, when Huck felt there was no percentage in Miss Watson's religion, but he didn't tell her so because it would only get her excited and wouldn't do any good. This feeling that certain things are useless because they don't do anybody any good is an indication of Huck's pragmatic leanings.

Our first hint of trouble comes when Huck talks about his father, "pap" as Huck calls him. From the fact that Huck doesn't believe his father drowned, we come to expect "pap" to show up any day.

CHAPTER 4.   THE HAIR-BALL ORACLE

Three or four months later, sometime in the winter, Huck is going to school, learning to read and write. The widow feels he is coming along slowly but surely, getting "sivilised." Huck is getting tolerant of his "new ways," his bed and clothes and food.

One morning, however, he sees a set of footprints in the snow outside the widow's house. He recognizes the cross made with big nails in the left boothill. His father is back in the village!

Huck runs to Judge Thatcher, the lawyer who has his money in trust for him, and sells the Judge his rights to both his share of the $12,000 and the interest (about $300 a year). The Judge gives Huck $1.00 for the money.

Then Huck goes to Miss Watson's slave, Jim, who has a magic hair-ball which he uses for telling fortunes. For a quarter (a counterfeit quarter, but Jim knows how to fix it by putting it between pieces of a raw potato) the hair-ball prophesies to Jim and Jim repeats to Huck. The "fortune" is this (Jim is telling Huck):

> "Yo' ole father doan' know yit what he's a-gwyne
> to do. Sometimes he spec he'll go 'way, en den
> agin he spec he'll stay. De bes' way is to res'
> easy en let de ole man take his own way. Dey's
> two angels hoverin' roun' 'bout him. One uv 'em
> is white en shiny, en t'other one is black. De

white one gits him to go right a little while,
den de black one sails in en bust it all up. A
body can't tell yit which one gwyne to fetch him
at ae las.' But you is all right. You gwyne to
have considerable trouble in yo' life, en considerable
joy. Sometimes you gwyne to git hurt, en sometimes you gwyne to git sick; but every time you's
gwyne to git well ag'in. Dey's two gals flyin'
'bout you in yo' life. One uv 'tm's light en t'other one is dark.
One is rich and t'other is po'.
You's gwyne to marry de po' one fust en de rich
one by en by. You wants to keep 'way fum de water
as much as you kin, en don't run no resk, 'kase it's
down in de bills dat you's gwyne to git hung."

Huck returns to the widow's house. When he goes up to his room at
night, he finds his father sitting there.

COMMENT: The story is beginning to get off the ground. Huck
seems to be changing, to be settling down to his new life. He has a
safe investment and is living in the home of a woman who loves
him with something very much like a mother's love. "She said
she warn't ashamed of me," is the way Huck recognizes this love.
But then, in the middle of what look like good days, Huck's father
appears. Huck is so frightened of his father that he sells out his
share of the wealth he and Tom found. He goes to Jim looking for
help from spirits, that is, Huck goes to Jim because Jim has a
reputation for his knowledge of spirits, witches, and devils. This
totally uneducated superstition seems to be the kind of religion Huck
trusts.

Be especially careful to note the "fortune." It doesn't tell Huck
what to do about his "pap," but it does tell him to stay clear of
the water. In the next couple of chapters we will see that the village
believes Huck was drowned. Then we will see Huck and Jim
escape on the river by means of a raft.

CHAPTER 5.   PAP STARTS IN ON A NEW LIFE

When Huck walks into his room, he doesn't see that his father is there
until after he shuts the door and turns around. With a shock he realizes
his father is sitting there, a very pale white ("a tree-toad white, a fish-belly
white," Huck says) with long, greasy black hair and long "mixed-up"
whiskers. He is wearing filthy rags and shoes through which his toes show.
Huck's father accuses him of putting on airs and "frills" in order to be
better than his family. He raves that since none of the family knew how to
read, Huck is being disrespectful in learning how to read. Pap tears up

a picture Huck received as a prize for his schoolwork, takes Huck's last dollar (the dollar Huck got from Judge Thatcher that morning), forbids Huck to go to school, and threatens to cause trouble for Judge Thatcher unless the Judge gives him Huck's share of the $12,000.

Because they want to protect Huck from his father, Judge Thatcher and the widow try to get him appointed their ward. That is, they want to be his legal guardians. But the court in the village has a new judge, one who is unfamiliar with Huck's pap. So this new judge decides not to separate Huck from his parent, because it's not a good thing to break up families. This decision boosts pap's pride and makes him so happy that he gets drunk on three dollars he forced Huck to borrow from Judge Thatcher. As a result of his spree the old man is jailed for a week. The new judge tries to reform pap by taking him into his house, cleaning him up, and making him respectable. Pap swears off liquor. He is welcomed into the new judge's family like a repentant sinner, and is given a spare room. But that night he gets thirsty, crawls out the window, trades his jacket for a jug of "forty-rod" (a cheap whiskey, something like "white lightning"), crawls back into his room, gets drunk, crawls out again, and breaks his left arm in two places. In getting drunk he practically destroys the spare room. The judge is disgusted with him.

> **COMMENT:**   In this chapter we get our first full-length view of Huck's father in action. Besides learning of his dirtiness and drunkenness, we are struck by the old man's meanness. We also note the peculiar pride he has in his ignorance and slovenliness. Just how Huck understands his relationship with his father is made clear when Huck says he continued to go to school after his father's appearance mainly in order to spite his father. The last picture we get of Huck's father in this chapter is that of a bedraggled, smelly drunk with a broken arm, lying helpless in the gutter. It looks as though the black angel of Jim's prophecy in the last chapter is going to win out.

CHAPTER 6.   PAP STRUGGLES WITH THE DEATH ANGEL

When pap gets well again, he begins chasing Huck and beating him for going to school. Huck borrows money from Judge Thatcher, gives it to pap who gets drunk, "tears up the town," and lands in jail.

Pap begins to hang around the widow's house, "laying for" Huck. When the widow tells him she'll make trouble for him, he threatens to show who's Huck Finn's boss. One spring day he catches Huck and takes him three miles up river to a log cabin in a thickly wooded spot on the Illinois shore, where nobody can find him.

Huck enjoys his captivity. For one thing, no one ever bothers him about studying or cleaning up. Life is carefree and lazy, except for the beatings Huck gets when his father is drunk. Huck accepts the beatings as part of life—for a while, at least.

But when pap takes to going off to town and locking Huck in the cabin for three or four days at a time, and when the beatings get more and more frequent, Huck decides he has to get away somehow.

One time while he is locked in the cabin, he finds an old, rusty saw blade which he uses in an attempt to cut his way through one of the logs at the back of the cabin. Pap comes back before he's free, so Huck hides his saw and disguises the log he's sawed through. Pap tells Huck that the widow and Judge Thatcher have another law suit against him, and it looks as though they'll win this time. Huck decides to escape before then, because he no longer wants to be civilized. He's too comfortable now to go back to the widow's. Then pap settles down to get drunk while Huck brings in the supplies and cooks supper.

The drunker pap gets, the more he "cusses" the government for treating him so badly while it lets freed Negroes vote. He gets so excited about what he's saying that he doesn't watch where he's walking. He trips over the salt pork tub, and curses louder and more violently while hopping up and down trying to soothe his barked shins. Finally he drinks himself into a stupor.

Huck manages to fall asleep for a while, but is awakened by a shriek. Pap is thrashing around yelling about snakes crawling over him. Then he shouts that he hears the footsteps of the dead. Then he thinks that Huck is the Angel of Death coming for him. He attacks Huck with an axe, but Huck runs around the cabin until pap gets tired and falls asleep. Huck takes down the gun, makes sure it's loaded, steadies it on the turnip barrel, aims it at pap, and waits for the dawn.

> **COMMENT:** It is in this chapter that we see Huck's resolve to escape. This escape is going to give rise to all his adventures: those on the river and off it. Huck's motives for wanting to escape are pretty clear: (1) he won't be safe with his father; (2) he can't tolerate "civilization"—not after the vacation from it he's taking now.

CHAPTER 7. I FOOL PAP AND GET AWAY

The next morning pap doesn't remember his struggle with the "death Angel," so Huck explains that he took the gun down because someone tried to break into the cabin. Pap sends Huck out to check the fish lines to see if they caught anything for breakfast. As he walks along the river bank, Huck notices the floating tree limbs and driftwood—a sure sign that the river is on the rise. Then he sees an empty canoe—13 or 14 feet long. He jumps into the river, clothes and all, and salvages it. Then he hides it in a little creek, thinking that when the time comes for his escape he'll use the boat to go about 50 miles downstream instead of hiking through the woods. He doesn't tell pap about the canoe, but explains his wet clothes by saying he fell in the river.

After breakfast, Huck and pap rest awhile. About noon they go out to see if anything of value is floating down the river. They get part of a raft—nine logs fastened together—which pap will take down to the village sawmill and sell. Huck is locked in again while pap goes to the village. He takes out his saw, and starts cutting away at the back of the cabin again. When he is free, he takes the sack of cornmeal, side of bacon, whiskey-jug, coffee and sugar, ammunition, wadding, bucket, gourd, dipper, tin-cup, the saw, two blankets, skillet, coffee-pot, fishlines, matches, and "everything that was worth a cent." All these things he puts in the canoe. Then he fixes up the ground he marked up crawling out of the hole when he dragged all these things out. He puts the log back in place so no one will be able to tell it has been cut through. Then he goes into the woods and shoots a wild hog; next, he takes the axe from the woodpile and smashes in the front door. He drags the pig into the cabin and hacks its throat with the axe so it will bleed all over the cabin floor. He drags a sackful of rocks over the ground to the river, so it will appear that something was dragged from the cabin and dumped in the river. Then he sticks some of his hair to the bloody axe and flings the axe into a corner of the cabin. He gets rid of the pig, then using the sack of corn meal, he leaves a false trail going away from river, so it will look as though someone carried a leaking sack of corn meal into the woods. Finally, Huck waits till dark, certain that when he leaves people will think he's been killed by robbers who escaped in the direction away from the river. He dozes for a while, and when he wakes it is late, and he sees pap rowing back from the village.

Huck sets his canoe adrift. Pretty soon he is passing the ferry landing where he can hear the distant voices of people talking, but they seem a long way off. Soon he can only hear a mumble and an occasional laugh as he lies in the bottom of the canoe, looking up at the deep sky.

He lands the canoe at Jackson's Island, where he hides it and lies down for a nap before breakfast.

COMMENT: This chapter is interesting in two ways. First, notice all the details involved in Huck's escape from pap. The kind of planning involved to make things appear as though Huck were killed by robbers is not the kind of planning we expect from Huck Finn. Instead, we think of Tom Sawyer as the kind of fellow who lays out this sort of plan. Huck realizes this, too. For just after he drags the pig and the rocks around, Huck says: "I did wish Tom Sawyer was there; I knowed he would take an interest in this kind of business, and throw in the fancy touches. Nobody could spread himself like Tom Sawyer in such a thing like that." The important thing to remember is that Tom would have done these things as a game; but Huck, on the other hand, does them in dead earnest.

Secondly, it is in this chapter that we get our first deep glimpse into Huck's feeling for the river. (In the second chapter, when the boys are on the hill overlooking the river, Huck mentions how beautiful the river is, but he doesn't explain himself, as he does here.) The river is awfully quiet, awfully strong, and awfully big—about a mile wide at this point. But you can hear a long way on it. You can, in a way, be part of what's happening on the shore (by listening), while you are separated from those happenings by a half-mile of water. When Huck, on Jackson's Island, hears the man on the lumber-raft give orders, he says with some surprise, "I heard that just as plain as if the man was by my side."

CHAPTER 8. I SPARE MISS WATSON'S JIM

Huck wakes up about eight o'clock feeling "powerful lazy and comfortable." Just as he's getting ready to turn over for 40 more winks, he hears a "boom!" up the river. It's the ferry boat, firing a cannon over the water to make Huck's body rise to the top. The people on the ferry boat set loaves of bread with quicksilver in them afloat on the river. The idea is that the loaves will come to a stop over the body. Huck is hungry, so he snags one of the loaves and eats it while he watches the boat full of villagers looking for his body. After rounding the island looking for the body, the boat with its occupants heads back to the village. Huck feels more secure now, in the knowledge that people believe he is dead and will no longer come looking for him.

For three days and nights Huck hangs around the island getting more and more bored and lonesome since he has nothing to do and no one to talk to. The next day he goes exploring on the island and stumbles across a smoldering campfire. In a panic he rushes back to his camp, packs his gear into the canoe, ready to be off and running on short notice, and climbs into a tree to hide. When he gets hungry, he goes across to the Illinois bank and cooks supper. His fear of the unknown person on the island keeps him from sleeping; so that night he decides to go looking for the other man. Once he makes this decision he feels better. He wanders a while until he comes to where he stumbled across the campfire. He sees a man sleeping beside the fire. When the man awakes, he stretches himself. Huck recognizes Miss Watson's Jim! Huck is so glad to see that the unknown person he feared is someone he trusts that he steps out of the woods and greets him. Jim is not so glad to see Huck. He had heard that Huck was dead, so he thinks that what he sees, is a ghost. Huck convinces Jim that he's not a ghost, and after providing breakfast for the two of them—Jim hasn't eaten anything but berries for at least four days—Huck tells Jim how he escaped from pap. Then Huck asks Jim what he is doing on the island. After making Huck promise not to tell on him, Jim says that he has run away from Miss Watson. Huck is shocked. Jim reminds him of his promise:

> "But mind, you said you wouldn' tell—you know you
> said you wouldn' tell, Huck."

> "Well, I did. I said I wouldn't, and I'll stick to
> it. Honest *injun*, I will. People would call me a
> lowdown Abolitionist and despise me for keeping mum—
> but that don't make no difference. I ain't a-going
> to tell, and I ain't a-going back there, anyways."

Jim explains that he ran away because he overheard Miss Watson tell the widow that a New Orleans slave trader offered her $800 for him. Although she didn't like the idea of selling a slave down the river (where slaves were less humanely treated than they were higher north), the amount of money was too much for her to turn down.

After telling Huck how he managed to escape and of the hardships he encountered on the island, Jim notes some omens, or superstitious signs, and tells Huck about some of the many signs and omens he knows. He tells Huck that his hairy arms and breast means he will be rich someday. As it is, he is worth $800, and he wishes he could spend some of it.

COMMENT: Huck feels secure when he sees the ferry boat give up the search for his remains. He points out that the bread had been prayed over by the widow or the parson so that it would find him. It found him—Huck ate it. The prayers were answered, Huck figures, because the right kind of people did the praying. Notice the irony here. Huck doesn't say that the purpose of the bread being set afloat was to find his body so it could be buried. What Huck seems to be telling us is that whether your prayers are answered or not depends on how you look at things.

The most important event in this chapter, though, is Huck's promise to Jim. Huck, wilfully and with full knowledge of the consequences of his promise, places himself outside the social order. He can't go back to the village (society) now, because he will protect a runaway slave. Huck is really "dead" now, so far as society is concerned.

CHAPTER 9.   THE HOUSE OF DEATH FLOATS BY

Against Huck's wishes, he and Jim carry their gear up to a cave in a 40-foot ridge on the island. The cave is high enough for Jim to stand up in, and as big as two or three rooms of a house. It has an outcropping beyond the opening so that Huck and Jim can build a fire. In a little while the sky starts to darken up, and it begins to thunder and lightning. Huck is impressed by the beauty of the stormy weather, especially when the wind whips the tree-tops and the lightning illuminates them for a flash. Jim reminds him that if he had been left to his own devices, he would still be down on the island, soaking wet in this storm.

The river continues to rise and to bring with it debris from flooded areas farther north. One night Huck and Jim catch a raft of pine planks, 12 by 16 feet, solid and well built.

Another night, just before daylight, they see a two-story frame house floating down the river. They paddle out to it, and find a dead man in it, shot in the back. The floor of the house is littered with whiskey bottles, greasy playing cards, and masks made out of black cloth. Jim and Huck ransack the house for candles, knives, tin-cups, and other materials they can use. Then they set off for their island again. By this time it is daylight. Jim has to hide in the bottom of the canoe covered with an old bedquilt taken from the house, while Huck paddles back to the island. They get home safe.

> **COMMENT:**   In this chapter Huck and Jim share their first common experience on the river. This new partnership between these social outcasts is rewarding to both parties. Huck, by allowing himself to be advised by Jim, is saved the loss of all his gear in the storm and the flooding which follows it. Jim finds equipment in the house floating down the river.
>
> The dead man in the house turn out to be Huck's pap, as we learn in the very last chapter of the novel. That is the reason why Jim didn't want Huck to enter the house until the dead man's face was covered. One other item was picked up out of the river by Huck and Jim: the raft. It is on this raft—a gift of the river—that the two will make their journey.

CHAPTER 10.   WHAT COMES OF HANDLIN'
SNAKE-SKIN

Huck and Jim have breakfast and then settle down to inspect their haul. Huck wants to know something about the dead man, but Jim says it's bad luck to talk about the dead, especially since they might come to haunt. They find $8 sewed in the lining of a coat they took from the house, and Huck begins to boast of their good luck. Two days earlier Huck had handled a snake-skin. Jim told him it was bad luck. Huck now says he wishes he could have more bad luck like that. Jim replies that the bad luck is yet to come.

Four days later Huck kills a rattlesnake and as a joke coils the snake up on the foot of Jim's blanket. Unknown to Huck, the rattlesnake's mate coils up on the blanket, next to the dead snake. When Jim lies down that night he is bitten by the snake. For four days and nights his foot and leg are swollen, and he is out of his head from the pain and from the whiskey he drinks to ward off the poison.

Finally the river begins to go down between its banks again. The first thing Huck and Jim do is bait a line with a skinned rabbit. They catch a catfish six feet two inches long, weighing over 200 pounds. It's as big a fish as was ever caught in the Mississippi.

The next morning Huck decides to go into the village to see what's happening there. Jim has him go at night, disguised as a girl, in some of the clothes they took from the floating house. Huck notices a light in the window of an old shack that had been abandoned last time he was in the village. He peeps in at the window and sees a 40-year old woman there, knitting. She is a stranger, who never met him. He reminds himself to behave like a girl, then knocks at the door.

COMMENT: The dominant theme of this chapter is superstition. The luck of finding the rich haul in the house and the luck of catching the huge catfish are balanced against Jim's snakebite. Just as Jim foretold the heavy rains by watching the flight of birds, so he foretells the snakebite by noting that it's bad luck to touch snake-skin with bare hands. Huck is repentant and vows never to touch snake-skin again.

Notice how neither Huck nor Jim distinguish between what is probable and what isn't. One might be able to tell something about the weather by watching the flight of birds. But handling snake-skin does not necessarily mean one is going to have bad luck.

Mark Twain uses superstition in three ways. First of all he uses it to indicate that the characters are plain, simple folks in the sense of being primitive and therefore uncluttered with a great deal of thinking through to the reality of things. The people are crude, but they are sincere and honest and innocent.

Secondly, Twain makes comic use of superstition. This book was written by a writer who gloried in being called "America's funny man." The comic element of *Huckleberry Finn* is a very important one, although it is often overlooked because of its obviousness. Twain uses humor, low comedy, satire, all to good effect.

Thirdly, the element of superstition is used to carry the theme of Fate through the novel. Instances of this use of superstition are the snakeskin, and Jim's belief that a hairy chest indicates future wealth.

CHAPTER 11. THEY'RE AFTER US!

The woman invites Huck into the house. He tells her his name is Sarah Williams and he's from Hookerville, a little village seven miles below St. Petersburg. He and the woman get to talking. She tells him all about the murder of Huck Finn, and how the village folk at first thought pap had killed his son to get the $6,000 from Judge Thatcher without having to go through the courts for it. But when the villagers discovered Jim had run away, they then suspected him. Then Huck's father borrowed money from Judge Thatcher to outfit a search party to look for Huck's killer. Then pap disappeared. A reward of $300 is posted for Jim, and one for $200 is posted for pap. The woman tells Huck she thinks Jim is hiding out on Jackson's Island because she saw smoke rising from there a few days ago. Her husband has gone off to get a boat and a gun. He and a friend are going to the island tonight to capture Jim.

Huck gets nervous and gives himself away—the woman discovers that he is not a girl. He tells her that he is an orphan apprenticed to a mean farmer and that he has run away. She sympathizes with him, explains some things he should do to act more like a girl, and sees him off.

Huck hears the clock strike eleven. In an hour the woman's husband will be going to the island to fetch Jim. Huck heads for the island, wakes Jim, and they load their gear on the raft and glide silently off down the river.

> COMMENT: The adventure on the Mississippi river—one of the most fascinating voyages in literature—is about to begin.

CHAPTER 12. BETTER LET BLAME WELL ALONE

Huck and Jim escape down the river on the raft, towing the canoe after them. Huck started a camp-fire on the island to decoy the men who were hunting Jim. He says, "I played it as low down on them as I could." They run all night and rest up during the day, watching the rafts and steamboats going up and down river. Jim fixes up the raft, making a kind of wigwam on it to keep out the weather and a fire-box so they can keep warm in cold and sloppy weather. The fifth night out they pass St. Louis, and five nights after that they spot a steamboat "that had killed herself on a rock."

Huck is gripped by a spirit of adventure and wants to investigate the boat. Jim doesn't want to go, but Huck argues and wins. Huck wishes Tom Sawyer were there, to enjoy the adventure.

When they board the steamboat, they discover that someone else is on it. There are three bandits on the boat, two of whom are about to kill their partner for threatening to squeal on them. The two decide not to shoot their partner, but rather to maroon him on the boat and let him drown when the boat breaks up. The reason is that to shoot the man would get them hanged, and besides "it ain't good morals."

Huck decides to cut the robbers' boat loose and maroon them all until he can get a sheriff to come and get them. At this point Jim discovers that the raft has broken loose.

> **COMMENT:** This chapter is full of references to the idyllic life Huck and Jim are living. They float down the river, stopping here and there to buy some supplies or "borrow" a chicken or watermelon or pumpkin. When they meet adventure, Jim tells Huck "Better let blame' well alone." But Huck, in the spirit of idealized adventure which is characteristic of Tom Sawyer, must seek out adventure. The gang of robbers that he runs into on the steamboat is the real thing. With them there is no such thing as bribing one of the gang who threatened to squeel—they will kill him. Compare Tom Sawyer's gang to this. Tommy Barnes (in Chapter Two) was lucky that Tom Sawyer only played make-believe.

CHAPTER 13.   HONEST LOOT FROM THE "WALTER SCOTT"

Unless Huck and Jim find the robbers' skiff, they too will drown with the robbers. After a tense search they find the skiff, but before they can get in it, two of the robbers come out, throw some loot in it, and get in themselves, preparing to leave their comrade to his death. But one of the two remembers that the man in the steamboat still has his share of the money, so they go back in to get it. Huck and Jim take advantage of their absence to scramble into the skiff and cut loose from the wreck. The swift current takes them quickly out of sight of the wreck. Then Jim takes to the oars, and sets off trying to catch up with their raft. As they glide rapidly along, Huck has time to stop and think. He begins to worry about the robbers, and "how dreadful it was, even for murderers, to be in such a fix." So he decides to have Jim put him ashore at the first light, and he will send help to the wreck, then meet Jim later, down river. But the plan doesn't work, because they catch up with the raft before they see a light on the shore. After they transfer the robbers' loot to the raft Huck takes the skiff and goes to a ferry slip nearby. He talks the captain of the ferry into going out to the wreck by telling him there are relatives of a rich man on board it. Before the ferry can get to the wreck, however, Huck sees the wreck floating down the river, breaking up. Huck feels sure the robbers are dead.

By the time Huck gets back to the raft, it is beginning to get light, and so he and Jim hide the raft on an island, sink the skiff, and sleep "like dead people."

> **COMMENT:** The elements of drama, suspense, and adventure dominate this chapter. The action is swift, the pace of the narrative is rapid—as rapid as the current that bears Huck and Jim away from the wreck.
>
> This chapter and the one before it provide a further contrast between Huck Finn and the world around him. Once again he meets people who lack any quality of humanity. In resolving to send some kind of help to the robbers, Huck shows a moral sense far superior to that of any character he's met so far. Neither the ferry captain nor the woman in St. Petersburg think of doing good unless some immediate reward is forthcoming. Huck alone seems not to put a price on his efforts.
>
> The *Walter Scott* is a den of thieves. This name is an indication of what Mark Twain thought of romantic novelists. (See COMMENT on *Life on the Mississippi*.)

CHAPTER 14.   WAS SOLOMON WISE

When they awoke, Huck and Jim sorted out the goods that the gang stole from the wreck. They found boots, blankets, books, clothes, cigars— all sorts of things. They lounge around all afternoon, talking and lazing. Huck tells Jim about the conversations he overheard on the steamboat, and says that this kind of thing is real adventure. Jim says he'd rather do without adventures, because when he discovered that the raft was missing he thought he was either dead or sold down river for sure. Huck reflects: "Well, he was right; he was most always right; he had an uncommon level head for a nigger."

He reads to Jim about kings and dukes and people like that, and they get into a discussion about the only example they both are familiar with: King Solomon. Jim doesn't think much of Solomon because Solomon didn't know that cutting a child in half doesn't answer the question about who the child belongs to. When Huck comes to understand that

Jim can't be reasoned with on this subject, he changes the topic to French kings. This leads to a discussion of the French language. Jim argues that Frenchmen ought to speak English like everybody else. At this point Huck gives up.

> **COMMENT:** In this chapter we see Huck feeling superior to Jim. Huck with his white man's education and "civilized" outlook doesn't understand Jim's reasoning, even though he realizes (in the beginning of this chapter) that Jim has practical common sense. Huck is still an adherent to the standards of his surroundings. We shall see him learn this, and try to change himself in the next few chapters.

> Of course, the humor in this chapter is obvious. It is based on Twain's device of contrasting appearance with reality: Jim's literalness and the spirit of things in this case.

CHAPTER 15. FOOLING POOR OLD JIM

Huck and Jim decide that they will travel on the raft to Cairo, Illinois, where the Mississippi River joins the Ohio River. There they'll sell the raft and take passage on a steamboat up the Ohio to the Free States. They figure they'll be in Cairo in three days.

On the second night they run into a heavy fog which causes them to tie up. Huck takes a line from the raft and paddles ahead in the canoe to find something to tie to. The current is so swift that the raft tears out the sapling he'd tied it to; Huck in the canoe is separated from Jim on the raft. Before Huck can take out after the raft, the fog closes in so thickly that he can't see 20 yards ahead of him. For the greater part of the night Huck and Jim shout to each other trying to locate themselves. When they become further separated by a group of small islands and swirling currents, they both become exhausted and fall asleep. Huck wakes up under a clear, bright night sky in the wide river. He sets out to look for the raft, and after being misled by floating debris finally finds it. Jim is still sleeping, and the deck of the raft is covered with dirt, leaves and other "rubbage." Seeing the condition of the raft, Huck thinks of the difficult time Jim must have had.

Nonetheless, Huck tries to fool Jim into thinking that there wasn't any fog, that they weren't separated, and that all that Jim went through was only a dream. Jim is convinced that it was all a bad dream, and he proceeds to interpret it. Huck then asks Jim to interpret the meaning of the debris that covers the deck.

Jim is abashed and taken back. He tells Huck that the joke isn't funny, since he was really afraid only for Huck's welfare in the fog. He says:

"Dat truck dah is *trash;* en trash is what people is dat puts dirt on de head er dey fren's en makes em ashamed." He gets up and walks to the wigwam.

Huck continues: "But that was enough . . . It was fifteen minutes before I could work myself up to go and humble myself to a nigger; but I done it and I warn't ever sorry for it afterward, neither."

> **COMMENT:** In this chapter Huck Finn seems to grow to the realization of what friendship is. He pulls a trick on Jim similar to the trick Tom Sawyer pulled on Jim in Chapter Two. Jim, as he did in Chapter Two, explains and "dresses up" the adventure he met with. But this time Huck is around to see the results of "playing games" with other people's feelings. He resolves not to play these tricks any more.
>
> In addition, Huck realizes that he must right the wrong he has done. And although it is against everything he has ever learned about relations between white men and Negroes (let us always remember that Mark Twain is portraying a small boy born and raised in the South during the 1830's), Huck humbles himself to Jim. This is Huck's first real victory over himself. He is now really better than his father—remember how pap cussed because a free Negro could vote?—because he puts aside all the conventional notions of relations between men, and begins to treat Jim with the dignity that belongs to a human being. Huck is the real idealist. Tom Sawyer only plays at romantic games.
>
> But Huck's trials and his growth are not over, not by a long shot.

CHAPTER 16. THE RATTLESNAKE-SKIN DOES ITS WORK

When they set out the next morning, Huck and Jim follow a big raft downstream. They're full of excitement about getting to Cairo. Huck begins to feel guilty because he's helping a slave to escape. Miss Watson never did him any harm, Huck thinks. And here *he* is, helping her property get away. He feels even more guilty when he hears Jim's plans for buying his wife out of slavery, and for stealing his children if their owner won't sell them. Huck feels that Jim will be doing an injustice by stealing his children. Huck is highly sensitive to the fact that he is helping Jim. And when Jim tells Huck his plan for stealing the children, Huck adds to himself, "I was sorry to hear Jim say that, it was such a lowering of him."

Huck decides to tell on Jim. His opportunity arises when he sets out in the canoe to check on their location. Before he's very far from the raft, he meets two armed men in a skiff who ask if he's seen any runaway slaves. Huck tries to squeal on Jim but can't, because he remembers that Jim called him "de bes' fren' Jim's ever had; . . . . de on'y white genlman dat ever kep' his promise to ole Jim." Because the men suspect Huck of hiding slaves on the raft, they decide to search it. Before they get to it, however, Huck gives them the impression that there's a man with smallpox on board. They back off rapidly, but give Huck $40 (which they put on a piece of driftwood that floats to him).

Huck goes back to the raft, "feeling bad and low" because he didn't do right—that is, he didn't turn Jim in. But then he thinks that if he had turned Jim in, he'd feel just as bad as he does now.

He finds Jim hiding in the water with just his nose sticking out, and calls him up. They figure they have about 20 miles to go, and that won't take them too long to cover. Then they'll be in Cairo, where they'll catch a steamboat heading North.

But the bad luck of the snake-skin catches up with them once more. During the foggy night they had passed Cairo, and are now miles downstream, heading deeper into slave territory. Downhearted and dejected, they decide to abandon the raft and take the canoe—which can be paddled against the current—upstream to Cairo. They discover that the canoe has broken loose from the raft. More bad luck from the snake-skin!

The only thing to do now is to continue downstream on the raft until they come to a place where they can buy a canoe to go North in. So, after dark, they set off again. The night is murky and gray, and so they light their lantern when they see a steamboat approaching them. The steamboat pilot apparently doesn't see the raft, and so he runs it down. As Huck dives overboard on one side of the raft he sees Jim go overboard on the other side. The steamboat slashes straight up the center. Huck dives deep to escape the paddlewheel. When he comes to the surface, he calls for Jim, but doesn't get an answer. Huck manages to get to shore. After "poking along" for about a quarter of a mile, he comes upon an old-fashioned log hut. Before he can run by and get away from it, he is cornered by a pack of dogs. So he stands still, very still.

COMMENT: In the early part of this chapter, Mark Twain makes use of irony, that is, his characters say one thing, when Twain himself obviously means to call our attention to the exact opposite. This irony is in the scene where Huck thinks of Jim, his wife, and children as the property of other people. The fact that Jim's children belong to some other person seems quite right, natural, and proper to Huck. Yet, by making so much of the point, by emphasizing it the way he does, Twain suggests to us how unjust it is that a man should be "lowered" by having to "steal" his children in order to keep his family together. People consider—as Huck Finn here considers—the injustice to the slave-owner, but not the injustice to the slave.

Huck, in feeling guilty about helping Jim escape, is still a child of his time. He is aware of right and wrong as his society explains it to him. He has a long way to go, and many adventures to experience before he finally matures as a man who can think for himself and withstand the social pressures which result in injustice. That he is moving in the right direction is made clear when he tells us that if he were to turn Jim in, he would feel just as bad as he does because he doesn't turn Jim in. Huck feels himself caught between two devils. He feels that men should stick together and help one another in times of trouble. He feels that to turn Jim in after he has given Jim his word not to, and after Jim has suffered a great deal for him, would be the last act of cowardice. As outcasts on the river they must support each other.

The bad luck that comes of handling snake-skin finally comes upon them in all its terrible force. Not only do the refugees overshoot Cairo, but they lose their canoe and raft, and they lose contact with each other. (We spoke—in the last paragraph—of men helping each other in times of trouble. Notice that the steamboat doesn't bother to stop to help any survivors after it smashes the raft.) In terms of the narrative thread, or plot of the story, this superstition makes a series of events believable which would otherwise seem merely coincidental.

CHAPTER 17.   THE GRANGERFORDS TAKE ME IN

The noise of the dogs awakens the occupants of the house, who greet Huck at the ends of their rifles. Cautiously they let him into the house and search him before they give him dry clothing and food. Huck tells them he fell overboard off the steamboat, and invents a family background. He notices, in the meantime, that the Grangerford house is well decorated (with brass knobs instead of iron or wood ones, and paintings on the wall and the like) for a country home. He concludes that they are a "nice family." Huck describes Emmeline Grangerford, a daughter who died when she was fifteen years old. He describes her as a painter and a poet, but he notices that most of what she's painted and written has been sad, on the theme of death. She seemed to be very sentimental about dead people, the kind of girl you'd go to if you wanted to cry; and she was happy mainly in times of sorrow.

COMMENT: The Grangerfords are an aristocratic Southern family representative of the fine families of the Old South in the days before the Civil War. This chapter and Chapter 18 contain a great deal of ironic comment on the social elite of plantation life. Notice how Huck admires the decorations of the Grangerford house. Notice also that the decorations are mawkish, trite, and really tasteless. But Huck is also aware of one other item—the food is good, and there are bushels of it.

CHAPTER 18.   WHY HARNEY RODE AWAY
FOR HIS HAT

Huck describes the head of the house, Colonel Grangerford, in just the terms we would expect to be used in describing an old-time southern plantation owner. When he scowls, nothing goes wrong for a week. He is head of a large family—there are Bob and Tom and Buck, Miss Charlotte and Miss Sophia. In addition, three sons were killed and Emmeline died young. The family—together with cousins from miles around— gathers frequently for social calls. The colonel owns hundreds of acres of farmland, and well over 100 slaves. He is carrying on a feud with a neighboring aristocratic family, the Shepherdsons. We learn about this feud when Huck and Buck (who is Huck's age, about 13 or 14) who are out in the woods hunting, see Harney Shepherdson riding along on his horse. Buck shoots at Harney, but misses him and only knocks his hat off. Despite the fact that he has a clear target, Harney doesn't shoot back. Instead, he rides off after his hat. When Huck asks Buck why the shooting occurred, Buck tells him about the feud.

Huck describes how the Grangerfords go to church the following Sunday, carrying their rifles. They hear a very good sermon on brotherly love. On the way home they talk about theological subjects.

Later that Sunday, Miss Sophia asks Huck to go to the church and get her Bible for her. Huck doesn't know it, but the Bible has a note in it from Harney Shepherdson, the man Sophia is in love with. The note tells the hour when Harney and Sophia will elope, go across the river and be married.

That afternoon, the slave who is assigned to wait on Huck takes him out to the woods and leads him to a cleared spot. Huck looks around and finds Jim. The two are re-united, and Jim tells Huck that he has repaired the raft. They can be on their way again.

The next morning, when Huck wakes up, he learns that the Grangerfords have all ridden out to intercept Sophia and Harney before they can cross the river. He follows after and sees a gunfight in which Buck and his cousin Joe (who at this point are the last living male members of the Grangerford family) are cut down. The shooting, Huck tells us, "made me so sick I most fell out of the tree [where he was hiding]. I ain't a-going to tell *all* that happened—it would make me sick again if I was to do that. I wished I hadn't ever come ashore that night to see such things.

I ain't ever going to get shut of them—lots of times I dream about them." When it gets dark, Huck climbs down from his tree, finds Buck's body, covers its face, and goes to where Jim has the raft hidden. After a moment of panic when he doesn't see the raft because Jim has moved it to a place where they can move out swiftly, Huck finds Jim and the raft. They see out into the river—at this place a mile and a half broad—and Huck feels "free and easy and comfortable" again.

> **COMMENT:** In chapters 17 and 18 we are given a picture of life among civilized people. The theme of man's being inhuman to man is well developed. The proud, fierce Grangerfords and Shepherdsons fight over some incident that no one can now recall. They respect each other, but they kill each other. They go to church and hear sermons on brotherly love, then set ambushes for each other. The churchgoing incident illustrates the underlying problem and underscores it ironically.
>
> The love affair between Sophia and Harney reminds us of the love in Shakespeare's *Romeo and Juliet*. Both Romeo and Juliet were members of feuding families; the difference between Shakespeare's characters and Twain's is that Shakespeare's Romeo and Juliet died before they could enjoy their married life together.
>
> It is important to notice how Huck is happy when he gets to the river, the raft, and Jim again. The sordidness, the bloodthirstiness, and the cruelty and stupidity of these highly respectable families makes him feel sick inside.

CHAPTER 19. THE DUKE AND THE DAUPHIN COME ABOARD

Huck and Jim spend some quiet days and nights on the river, which are ended the morning that Huck picks up two men running from a mob of angry townspeople. They are obviously con-men who have been found out by their victims. Huck brings these men to the raft. The younger of the two men, about thirty years old, says he is the rightful claimant to the title of Duke of Bridgewater, but that he has been cheated out of his inheritance. He moans and sighs for awhile, until Huck and Jim offer to make him feel better by calling him by titles of respect ("Your Grace," and the like), and by waiting on him. By and by, it turns out that the other man, who is about seventy years old, is the rightful claimant to the throne of France, the Dauphin. The only way Huck and Jim can make *him* feel good is to call him "Your Majesty" and not sit until he tells them they can.

Huck realizes that the two men aren't really royalty, but he says nothing because it wouldn't pay. All he wants to do is keep peace in the family.

He adds, "If I never learnt nothing else out of pap, I learnt that the best way to get along with his kind of people is to let them have their own way."

> **COMMENT:** The idyllic journey Huck describes in the opening paragraphs of this chapter is about to be interrupted for good and all by the appearance of the king and the duke. The description of the river at daybreak is a song of appreciation of the simple beauty and goodness of Nature, marred only where it has been touched by the hand of man. Huck enjoys the stillness, the calm and the quiet of the river.
>
> Contrasted with this mood is the behavior of the king and duke, the two river characters who make their livings swindling the simple village folk.
>
> Huck's love for peace and quiet is further brought out in this chapter when, after he notices that the two men are frauds, he decides to keep quiet, because to do otherwise would only cause trouble. By keeping quiet about what he knows, Huck is in a favorable position so far as his dealings with the scoundrels are concerned. He knows they are frauds; they think he doesn't know. Beginning with this chapter the theme of Jim's escape from slavery is dropped into the background. It comes up later in the story where it forms the nucleus of the farcical escapade that Huck engages in with Tom Sawyer on the farm of Silas Phelps.

CHAPTER 20.   WHAT ROYALTY DID TO PARKVILLE

By asking them if they think a runaway slave would run South, Huck convinces the king and the duke that Jim is not a runaway. He then makes up a story about his family, telling them that Jim is the only piece of property he has left. The reason they run only at night, Huck says, is that too many people have tried to board the raft and take Jim, accusing him of being a runaway.

The king and the duke—being "royalty"—take over the beds in the raft's wigwam, leaving Huck and Jim to sleep outside. Huck notices how Jim stands watch for himself and Huck too. He understands that Jim is his friend.

Next day the duke proposes to put on *Romeo and Juliet* in the villages they run across. The king agrees with him, and sets about learning his parts. Later the king and the duke take Huck into a small village down around the bend. They discover from an old Negro that almost everybody is down at a prayer-meeting. Leaving the duke in the village's printing shop (which is empty, since the whole population went to the meeting), the king and Huck go to the prayer-meeting. There they hear a preacher delivering an emotional sermon. The king stands up and confesses that he is a pirate captain come from the Indian Ocean to find men for a crew. He cries and blubbers about his sins, and promises that he will raise money to go back and devote his life to missionary work among the pirates. The villagers, emotionally excited, take up a collection for him, netting him $87.75, and a three-gallon jug of whiskey he manages to steal from its resting place under a wagon.

The duke in the meantime had set up some jobs in the printing office and made money from people who thought he was the shop owner. In addition, he designed a poster advertising a reward for a runaway slave. Using this as evidence, he says, they can say that Jim is a runaway being returned to his rightful owner. That way the raft can be run in the daytime. All four agree that this is a good idea.

At four in the morning when Jim calls Huck to take the watches, he tells Huck he hopes they don't run into any more royalty. He doesn't like the two they have.

> **COMMENT:** In this chapter we are introduced to the workings of the frauds. They think nothing of breaking into people's confidence and making fools of the villagers. This behavior is the real-life extension of Tom Sawyer's make-believe and "game" playing.

CHAPTER 21. AN ARKANSAW DIFFICULTY

The duke undertakes serious rehearsals for the production of the balcony scene from *Romeo and Juliet.* He adds—for excitement—a sword fight scene from *Richard III* and Hamlet's soliloquy. He teaches the king a botched-up version of the soliloquy. One morning he goes into a little village where he gets handbills printed up announcing the presentation of the three scenes. On the handbills he represents himself as David Garrick, the Younger, and the king as Edmund Kean, the Elder.

They come across a little village which is being visited by a circus—a stroke of luck, they feel, since all the countryfolk will be coming into town for the circus, and so may stay for the Shakespearian presentation.

Huck describes the town and its inhabitants. The place is obviously a one-horse village. The streets are a foot deep in mud in places, and the villagers, like most Southerners of the period, are lazy ne'er-do-wells. As the town fills up with people coming in from the country, the villagers get more and more rowdy. Finally a country character named Boggs who has a reputation for threatening people but doing nothing about his threats comes into town.

He is high-spirited as a result of heavy drinking. He rides up to the biggest store in town and insults its owner, a Colonel Sherburn. Sherburn comes out of the store and tells Boggs he has until one o'clock to continue the insults. After that time Sherburn will hunt him down. At one o'clock Boggs is still "cussing." The villagers send for his daughter to calm him down. Before she can come, however, Sherburn finds Boggs and shoots him down in cold blood before the horrified eyes of the villagers and country-folk. Boggs is carried to the village drug store, where he dies surrounded by a crowd of curious onlookers. Witnesses to the action begin describing and acting it out to the latecomers. In a little while the crowd gets worked up, and somebody suggests lynching Colonel Sherburn. The mob takes up the cry, and storms toward Sherburn's house, snatching up clotheslines to do the hanging with.

> **COMMENT:** In this chapter Mark Twain describes the typical early nineteenth-century sleepy village in the South. Its laziness, slowness, dirt, and ignorance make it fit game for con-men like the king and duke who try to pass themselves off as once-famous British actors. By the 1830's, Garrick was long dead and Kean had recently died in 1833. The soliloquy which the duke teaches the king is obviously a half-remembered mish-mash of snatches of phrases from several of Shakespeare's plays. Notice how the duke seems to take over as the leader of the two frauds.
>
> Boggs doesn't insult Sherburn after one o'clock. Not only that, but Sherburn shoots Boggs twice. This makes it seem that Sherburn was deliberately trying to upset the calm of the village.
>
> Notice also that when Boggs dies, several of the villagers begin imitating Sherburn—one in particular is good at it. By describing the actions of the villagers before, during, and after the shooting, Twain gives us a picture of the mob which makes it seem to be made up of fools and cowards.

CHAPTER 22.   WHY THE LYNCHING BEE FAILED

The mob storms Sherburn's house, trampling the fence that stands in its way. Then Sherburn steps out on the roof of his porch with a shotgun in his hand. Scornfully he rebukes the crowd for its cowardliness in coming for him illegally instead of having him arrested. He points out the cowardice of the average man—in the North for allowing himself to be downtrodden, in the South for needing the protection of the mob in lynching parties. He singles out the leader of the mob—a person named Buck Harkness—whom he refers to as a half-a-man. Finally he orders the mob to disperse and "take your half-a-man with you."

Huck leaves too, and goes to the circus. He is impressed by the glitter of the parade, and when a "drunk" gets into the act and tries to ride a circus horse, Huck feels embarrassed for him. But it turns out that the "drunk" is a member of the troupe. Huck feels sorry for the ringmaster who, he says, was put upon by one of his performers.

That night the king and the duke put on their show, and draw twelve people who obviously don't appreciate their brand of Shakespeare. The duke makes up a sign advertising another show, "The Thrilling Tragedy of the King's Cameleopard or The Royal Nonesuch . . . Ladies and Children Not Admitted."

> **COMMENT:** The sudden fury of the mob and its equally sudden dispersal are illustrations of the totally herd-like quality of the villagers. The people behave like cattle who are easily led and easily frightened. Sherburn's speech is straightforwardly cynical; it thoroughly dispirits the mob and destroys its self-righteous anger. The fact that Huck is still a small village boy at heart is made clear in his comment about the ringmaster. Huck can't tell the difference here between showmanship and reality. He thinks the ringmaster was really fooled by the clown pretending to be a drunken country boy. It is obvious that the whole scene was part of the circus' entertainment. Huck can't be entertained by that kind of pretense.

CHAPTER 23. THE ORNERINESS OF KINGS

The next day the king and the duke put on their show. The audience, attracted by the last line of the handbill—"Ladies and Children Not Admitted"—is a large one. The show consists of the king hopping around the stage on all four, naked. When the duke announces that the show is over, the audience feels that it has been cheated and is about to attack the duke and the king. One man in the audience gets up and tells the rest that it wouldn't be smart to admit they were made fools of because they would be the laughing-stocks of the village. He tells the rest of the audience to go out and praise the show, getting the rest of the villagers to come. Then everyone in the village will be in the same boat. So the audience leaves peacefully. The second night the same thing happens. On the third night Huck stands near the door where the duke is collecting admissions. He notices that the crowd is much larger, made up of many people who have seen the show on one of the other two nights. He notices also the smell of "sickly eggs," "rotten cabbages and such things." The duke gives a bystander a quarter to tend the door while he goes backstage. Instead of going backstage, however, the duke and Huck head for the raft as fast as they can. Huck figures the king is in for trouble. But when they reach the raft and set out toward mid-stream, the king crawls out of the wigwam and asks them how things went. Huck is surprised to learn that he had never been to town. The king and the duke laugh over the stupidity of the townspeople who paid out $465.00 in the three nights, and were cheated out of their revenge.

When the king and duke fall asleep, Jim asks Huck if he isn't surprised by the way they carry on. Huck doesn't see any reason for telling Jim that the men aren't real royalty; it would do no good. Besides, he adds, you probably couldn't tell the real ones from these frauds.

Huck falls asleep, and Jim doesn't wake him when it's his turn to stand watch. When Huck awakens by himself at daybreak, he hears Jim bemoaning his children. Huck gets Jim to talking about his wife and family, and learns that Jim feels very bad because he once punished his little girl 'Lizabeth for not closing a door when he told her to. After he punished her, he discovered that she was deaf as a result of scarlet fever.

> **COMMENT:** The "orneriness" of human nature is the theme of this chapter. The king and the duke cheat the villagers by appealing to their lower appetites. The villagers cheat their neighbors in order not to appear foolish. Then all the villagers are left high and dry when they come back for revenge, because the duke is more clever than they are. Jim, alone, is aware that the king and the duke don't represent the ordinary run of human beings. Huck feels there is nothing you can do; they (people in general) are all alike. It isn't too difficult to see that Huck is here acting as a mouthpiece for Mark Twain, himself.
>
> Notice that Jim is remorseful when he's reminded of the incident of his daughter. In a poignant and touching confession he tells us that he can never forgive himself for being cruel to the poor deaf child, even though he wasn't really cruel, and he had no way of knowing beforehand that the child didn't hear him tell her to shut the door. Contrast the cruelty of Huck's pap with what Jim takes to be his own cruel action towards 'Lizabeth.

CHAPTER 24.   THE KING TURNS PARSON

The king and the duke plot to "work" the villagers on either side of the river where the raft is tied up. They can't decide on a "project"; they're afraid to try the "Nonesuch" because word might have leaked down from the last village they tried it in. So while the duke stays aboard the raft to scheme something up, the king takes Huck out in the canoe to see if he can make anything. The king directs Huck to head for a steamboat laying up about three miles above the town. Huck is happy because he wants a steamboat ride. But before they get to the boat, the king sees a country boy walking along the shore, and invites him into the canoe where he asks him questions about the village and everybody in it. The boy, innocent and unsuspicious, tells the king everything he knows. Among the things that he tells the king is the fact that Peter Wilks, a villager, just died, and the rest of the villagers are expecting his brothers—Harvey, a clergyman, and William, a deaf-mute—to arrive from England at any moment. The brothers will take over Peter's estate when they arrive and administer it for Peter's nieces, Mary Jane, Susan, and Joanna. The king learns that the country boy is going to New Orleans to take passage to South America. When they get to the steamboat, the king puts the country boy on it, and has Huck paddle him another mile up the river before sending Huck back to the raft to fetch the duke. Huck knows what's going to happen, but he doesn't let on. When Huck brings the duke back, the king explains that he plans to impersonate the brothers of the dead Peter Wilks. The duke will be the deaf-mute, and the king will be the preacher.

They flag down a big steamer and have it land them at the village. They go into the main street, with Huck as their servant, as though they don't know that Peter's dead. Upon learning that their "brother" is dead, the king and duke sob and cry and carry-on. Huck is disgusted. He says, "It was enough to make a body ashamed of the human race."

COMMENT: By playing on the innocence and inexperience of a country boy, the king and duke are about to attempt their biggest confidence fraud yet. They are counting on the ignorance of the townspeople and the emotional upset caused by their uncle's death to separate the girls from their proper inheritance. Huck is about to rebel against the atrocious behavior of the king and duke. The fact that he is disgusted with their trifling with human beings makes him steal from them in a later chapter.

Huck's disgust is also a reflection of Mark Twain's attitude toward fraud and inhumanity.

CHAPTER 25. ALL FULL OF TEARS AND FLAP DOODLE

The news of the arrival of Peter's "brothers" travels rapidly, and when they get to the house, they are greeted by an enthusiastic throng of villagers, together with the three girls. After making a great and public display of sorrow, the king and duke get down to their serious business—finding out how much money Peter had. Mary Jane, the eldest niece, hands over the letter Peter left, telling where the money is hidden. Three thousand dollars and the house are to be given to the girls, and three thousand dollars and George's tanyard—George is another brother, the girls' father; he died shortly before Peter did—are to go to the brothers. When the king and duke go down the cellar to get the money, they discover that $415 is missing. They do not want to appear dishonest, and so they make it up out of the money they made at "The Royal Nonesuch." To make a "splash" the king gives the money to the girls, saying he and his brother feel that since the girls are poor orphans they should have it all. While he's at it, he makes a speech which is interrupted by the village doctor, Doctor Robinson, who accuses him of being a fraud. But the townspeople are too firmly convinced that the king and duke are Peter's brothers. They argue and try to quiet him. Finally the doctor tells the girls not to trust the imposters. But Mary Jane shows her "spunk" by giving the king the $6,000, telling him to invest it for her and her sisters without giving them a receipt for it. The doctor again warns the townspeople and the girls of the foolish mistake they're making, and goes away.

> **COMMENT:** The hypocritical and inhumane dishonesty of Huck's "royalty" is made crystal clear in this chapter. Mark Twain strikes out at the blundering ignorance and the unthinking sentimentality of the villagers, and especially of the eldest of the three girls— Mary Jane—who, because of her sentimentalized hospitality, practically begs to be swindled.
>
> Doctor Robinson represents the rational element in the human race, the element Mark Twain came more and more strongly to identify himself with. This rational segment believes things only when documented proofs have been presented to it. It is probably no accident that this doctor has the same name as the doctor who was murdered while robbing a grave in *Tom Sawyer*. The reason the Doctor Robinson in *Tom Sawyer* was robbing graves is that he wanted bodies to experiment with and to dissect. Nowadays people will their bodies to medical schools for just such purposes, but in the nineteenth century and earlier it was usually considered criminal to dissect human cadavers. Hence, people who wanted to advance science and dispel ignorance had to get their materials any way they could.
>
> What is important to note is that Mark Twain sets up a conflict between the lone reasonable man and the crowd of unthinking, materialistic, sentimental common people.

CHAPTER 26.   I STEAL THE KING'S PLUNDER

The king and the duke intend to stay overnight in the girls' house, and so they ask Mary Jane for rooms. She puts Uncle William (the duke) in the spare room, Huck in the cubbyhole in the attic, and Uncle Harvey (the king) in her room, although it has her dresses and things hanging on the wall.

Huck eats supper that night with Joanna, the 14 year old who has a hare-lip. She asks him questions about England, and he blunders through her questioning with answers that are contradictory. She notices this, and accuses him of lying. Mary Jane and Susan (the 15 year old)

overhear this accusation and make Joanna apologize to Huck. Huck
feels "low and mean" because he's helping the king and duke steal their
money. He feels even worse because the girls are going out of their way
to make him feel at home and among friends. He wants to tell on the
king and duke, but he's afraid to go to the doctor because he doesn't want
word to get out about his telling. He feels he can't tell Mary Jane because
she's so honest—all her feelings show in her face. He decides to steal
the money.

After searching the duke's room and not finding the money, he goes to
the king's. Before he can search the room thoroughly, the sound of
footsteps sends him running for a hiding-place behind the dresses hanging
on the wall. He overhears a conversation between the king and duke,
in which the duke tries to convince the king that they should steal just
the $6,000, and run away in the middle of the night. But the king thinks
it's silly to run off with the cash and leave the money that can be gotten
from selling old Peter's property. He convinces the duke that they should
sell the house, tanyard, and slaves, and take all the money. They will say
they are taking the girls to England with them, and this will give them
the excuse they need to sell the property quickly. After they run off,
people will realize that the sales were illegal, and the girls will get their
property back.

The duke agrees to this. He cautions the king about hiding the money they
already have. The king takes the money from its hiding place among the
dresses—about a foot away from where Huck is hiding—and stuffs
it into the mattress. When they leave the room, Huck takes the money
up to his cubbyhole and waits for everyone in the house to fall asleep.
Then he slips quietly down the stairs.

COMMENT: The king's argument that the sales will be held to
be illegal and that the girls will get their property back is not realistic; it is a sign of his and the duke's greed. The duke gives in to
this false reasoning a little too easily. For although the girls may
get their property back, the proceedings involved are long and
costly.

Huck is touched by the girls' position as orphans and by their basic
goodness and unselfishness. He decides to help them. Notice how
Mark Twain has the action develop by means of a series of coincidences. Huck accidentally overhears the king and the duke hatch
their plot; he hides behind the dresses which are left in the room
for no specific reason; he doesn't hide under the bed because it
happens to be a low bed, and so he escapes getting caught. Using
coincidences like this is usually considered a flaw in a literary work.
But Mark Twain paces the action so swiftly that the flaw—if in
this instance it is one—is hardly noticeable. Not only that, but
he makes the coincidental action work for him by providing a way
to heighten the suspense.

CHAPTER 27. DEAD PETER HAS HIS GOLD

Huck tries to get outside to hide the money, but the front door is locked. Then he hears somebody coming. There is no place for him to go. He hides the money in the coffin, with Peter. After he tucks the money away and gets out of sight behind the door, he sees Mary Jane enter and kneel in front of the coffin and cry. He slips out of the room without being seen and goes back up to bed, where he lies awake all night worrying what to do next. He's afraid to go down and get the money out of the coffin because somebody might catch him. He's sure the money will be found when the undertaker screws the lid on the coffin. Then the king will have it, and there will be no second chance to steal it.

Finally the hour of the funeral comes, and as Huck sweats with worry over the money in the coffin, the undertaker slides the lid over Peter and screws it down. Now Huck is in a fix. He doesn't know whether the money is still in the coffin, or whether someone found it and took it away without mentioning it. Because he's unsure, he doesn't know whether there would be any use in writing Mary Jane a letter telling her that the money was put into the coffin.

That evening the king sets up the sale of the girls' property by telling people that he and William have to get back to England and want to take the girls with them. The girls are all excited, and can't wait to get going. However, their spirits are considerably dampened the next day when the king sells their Negroes to slave traders—the two sons up the river and the mother down the river. The girls think it was cruel of the king to separate the family. Huck consoles himself with the knowledge that the sale is illegal, and the family will be back together again shortly. But the townspeople are upset.

The next morning the king and duke notice that the money is missing from the king's mattress. They question Huck, who tells them that he's seen the slaves going in and out of the room, but didn't think anything of it at the time. He leads the two frauds to believe that the Negroes who were sold the day before may have taken the money with them. The duke blames the king for being so greedy that he sold the slaves off too quickly. If they were still around the house, he argues, the money would be, too. The king and duke argue for a while; then the king curses Huck and himself for not understanding what the slaves were doing.

> COMMENT: The humorous situation concerning the noises in the basement during the funeral service provides Huck with an opportunity to admire the calmness and composure of the under-taker. Note how easily the crowd is distracted from the immediate proceedings, and note also how the undertaker is careful to satisfy the crowd's curiosity.

CHAPTER 28. OVERREACHING DON'T PAY

Next morning as Huck is going downstairs, he hears Mary Jane crying in her room while she's packing for the trip to England. He asks her what's bothering her, and she tells him that she's upset over the inhuman treatment shown the slaves. He blurts out that the family will be reunited within two weeks. She wants him to repeat what he's just said, and he does. But first he makes her promise to leave the house that very morning, before breakfast, and visit friends for three or four days. He's afraid the truth will show on her face, and people will force her to tell them; then he and Jim will be in trouble.

He outlines a plan to her. She will stay at her friends' house outside town until 9:00 or 9:30 that night. Then she'll came back and put a candle in the window. If Huck doesn't show up by eleven, she's to have the king and the duke jailed. If Huck is to get caught, she's to have him released. In order to make sure the king and the duke get jailed as frauds Huck gives her a slip of paper with "Royal Nonesuch, Bricksville" written on it. He tells her to send to Bricksville to find out all she needs to know about the frauds. As he's seeing her off, he gives her another note telling her where he put the money.

Huck explains Mary Jane's absence to Susan and Joanna by saying she went across the river to visit some sick friends. He warns them not to tell the king and duke why she went because that would only postpone the trip to England—they would be quarantined because the illness is catching. Instead he suggests that they tell the "uncles" their sister went across the river to convince some friends to come to the auction and buy the house.

At the auction that afternoon the king and duke sell off everything. While they're selling the last item—a graveyard plot—a steamboat lands two men who claim to be Peter Wilks' brothers.

> **COMMENT:** Compare Huck's plan for saving the girls' fortune with Tom Sawyer's plan for liberating Jim in Chapter 34 and following. Huck's plans are simpler, more realistic than Tom's. This is an important way in which the boys differ. Huck is concerned with results, Tom with methods.
>
> It is important to note that the greed of the king and duke gets them into trouble—and this trouble could land them in the penitentiary.

CHAPTER 29. I LIGHT OUT IN THE STORM

The two men who claim to be Peter's brothers are "nice looking." The one who claims to be Harvey is older than the other, who has his arm in a sling. They say they will wait tlll their baggage comes in to prove they are who they say they are. The doctor and the lawyer (Levi Bell, who has just returned from a business trip) and a man named Hines (he saw the king and Huck pick up the country boy) side with the newcomers and claim that the king and duke are frauds. The king denies this. He argues that the newcomers are frauds. After some inconclusive argument, the old gentleman asks the king to describe the tattoo on Peter's breast. The king thinks quickly and says it's a thin blue line you can't see if you don't look closely. The newcomer says it's a small, dim P-B-W. Since the men who laid Peter out for burial didn't see either the line or the P-B-W, Levi Bell suggests they all go down to the graveyard and dig Peter up. The crowd collars all four men and Huck, and heads for the cemetery. It is now dark, and beginning to thunder and lighten, and rain begins to fall. In a flash of lightning somebody sees the bag of gold and sings out. The man who is holding Huck jumps forward for a look and, in the excitement, releases him. Huck escapes. As he is running through town he sees a light flash in Mary Jane's window, and his heart swells up. He gets to the river and takes a canoe. He heads for the towhead in midriver where the raft is tied up. As he jumps aboard the raft, he tells Jim to cut loose—they're free of the king and the duke.

His joy is short-lived, however, for while he's dancing around he hears the sound of oars. The lightning shows him the king and the duke heading for the raft. "So I wilted right down onto the planks, then, and give up; and it was all I could do to keep from crying."

> **COMMENT:** The element of coincidence saves not only Huck and the king and the duke, but it also saves the girls' money. Were it not for the coincidental arrival of the real brothers, the king and duke might have got clean away. But the newcomers arrived at the last possible moment; even the reader has stopped expecting them to show up. And were it not for the tattoo which nobody noticed, the men wouldn't have been taken to the graveyard. And of course the sudden thunderstorm is the perfect weather for digging up corpses in.
>
> When the king is confronted with the question of the tattoo on Peter's breast, he brashly attempts to bluff it out. In the next chapter the duke is going to praise the king for this sudden inspiration. In what kind of person is such quick thinking praiseworthy? This kind of bluff is an important part of the king's character.
>
> Throughout the chapters dealing with the Wilks affair, Huck has a feeling for the girls—particularly Mary Jane—quite unlike his feelings for any one else in the book. His feeling for Jim is different, as is his feeling for Aunt Sally (see chapters 40, 41). He admires Mary Jane's "spunk" or "sand." We suspect he might fall

in love with her if he were a different sort of fellow. Notice how the vagueness and inexactness of the word "sand" in this context is precisely the kind of vagueness one expects from a boy like Huck in this situation.

CHAPTER 30. THE GOLD SAVES THE THIEVES

When the king and the duke get aboard the raft, the king shakes Huck, accusing him of trying to run out on them. But the duke tells the king to let Huck alone—neither the king nor the duke stopped to save Huck when they got their opportunities to escape from the crowd. So they have no reason to expect that Huck would look around and try to save them when his chance came.

The two frauds begin to argue about the money. They have not only lost the Wilks fortune, but they lost the money they made from the "Royal Nonesuch" to boot. They accuse each other of stealing the money and hiding it in the coffin. Huck is uneasy, until the duke forces the king to confess that he stole it. The king confesses—an outright lie, because we know Huck stole it—only after the duke takes him by the throat and throttles him. After this incident, the men curl up with their whiskey, and within a half hour they are friendly again.

COMMENT: This chapter does two things: it develops the characters of the king and the duke, and it serves as a transition between the Wilks episode and the next affair. Note how the king tries to take out his anger on Huck; note how the duke confesses that he planned to steal the money, and forces a similar confession from the king. The duke bullies the king just as the king bullied Huck. Compare the results of this adventure with the king's boast earlier that he likes to trust to "Providence." He ends up losing money instead of making it.

CHAPTER 31. YOU CAN'T PRAY A LIE

After lying low for a while, the king and duke begin stopping at villages again, but with little success. Their attempts at running dancing schools, prayer meetings, temperance clinics, and the like meet with failure. Huck notices that they are broke and desperate. They plot and scheme together for two and three hours at a time. He and Jim decide to rid themselves of their royalty the first chance they get. One morning they stop near a little village called Pikesville, where the king goes ashore to see if the people have heard of "The Royal Nonesuch." He says that if he isn't back by noon, the duke and Huck are to come into town.

The king doesn't come back by noon, and so the duke and Huck go into town where they find the king drunk. While the king and duke are arguing,

Huck runs back to the raft figuring that while the frauds are fighting he and Jim will make their getaway.

When he goes to the raft, he finds that Jim is gone. He shouts for him and searches the woods, but can't find him. Heartbroken by what he fears has happened to Jim, he sits down and cries.

After a while he goes out onto the road where he sees a boy walking. He asks the boy whether he's seen a man fitting Jim's description. The boy says he has seen a runaway slave who was taken to Silas Phelps' farm. It seems the king told Phelps that Jim is a runaway from below New Orleans, and that there is a $200 reward for him. The king sells his interest in the reward to Phelps for $40, because he is in a hurry to go up river and can't wait around for the owner to come and claim Jim.

Huck is grieved by the doublecross the king and the duke pulled on Jim. He decides that Jim would be better off at Miss Watson's than down river, and so he resolves to write a letter to Tom Sawyer telling him to inform Miss Watson of Jim's whereabouts. But he reconsiders. He knows that Jim would be despised because he ran away, and would probably be sold down river anyway. Also, he thinks that everybody will find out that he helped Jim escape. He wouldn't be able to face his friends.

He decides to reform himself. He kneels down and tries to pray, but can't find words—because he wasn't really going to give Jim up. So he writes the letter, and immediately feels better. Before he prays, however, he begins thinking of all the good and bad times he and Jim shared on the river. He remembers that Jim called him "the only friend ol' Jim ever had." He thinks: If ever Jim needed a friend, he needs one now. His eye lights on the letter he has just written. He thinks to himself:

> "It was a close place. I took it up, and held it in my hand. I was a-trembling, because I'd got to decide, forever, betwixt two things, and I knowed it. I studied a minute, sort of holding my breath, and then says to myself: 'All right, then, I'll go to hell'—and tore it up. It was awful thoughts and awful words, but they was said. And I let them stay said; and never thought no more about reforming."

Huck decides to go to work to steal Jim out of slavery again. He hides the raft on an island. The next morning he dresses in his good clothes, eats, bundles some belongings and goes ashore in the canoe. He hides his bundle and canoe and begins walking toward Silas Phelps' place. Before he gets there, he meets the duke who is putting up "Royal Nonesuch" posters. He tells the duke a story about the raft being lost—pretending he thought the king and the duke took Jim and ran off without him the day before. The duke explains that the king sold Jim and spent the $40 drinking and gambling. The duke is obviously afraid that Huck might expose the "Royal Nonesuch" fraud, and so he gives him directions to a non-existent farm forty miles away. Huck pretends to believe him and sets out in the direction the duke points. But he doubles back through the woods toward the Phelps place. He wants to get to Jim and tell him to keep mum about the "Royal Nonesuch." He is afraid of what the frauds might do to anyone who squeals on them.

> **COMMENT:** In this chapter Mark Twain again takes up the story of Jim's escape from slavery. He has left it alone for a while in order to recount the adventures of the king and the duke. The entire emphasis of this section of Jim's story will be different from what it was before, as we shall see in the following chapters.
>
> Huck's moment of crisis comes when he finally resolves to follow his heart instead of his head. He will save Jim—which is, as far as he is concerned, wrong. He has been taught that the right thing to do is to turn Jim in. This chapter restates with emphasis the theme of chapters 15 and 16, in which Huck arrives at the same conclusion. Huck's determination not to unsay what he has said is a clear indication of his basic honesty and integrity. Whatever he is—Abolitionist, or worse—he is not a hypocrite. "You can't pray a lie," he says. He might like to do wrong and get away with it; but since that obviously won't work, he isn't going to do right for the wrong reason. He decides, and accepts the consequences of his decision: " 'All right, then, I'll go to hell'—. . . . It was awful thoughts and awful words. . . ."
>
> For all his courage in making this resolution, note that he is nevertheless reluctant to cause trouble for the king and the duke. This is not because he likes the two frauds, but, rather, because he wants to keep out of trouble so he can work out Jim's escape.

CHAPTER 32.   I HAVE A NEW NAME

When Huck gets to the Phelps farm, he finds that it is "one of these little one-horse plantations, and they all look alike." He describes the place in some detail. Before he gets to the house, however, he is surrounded by yammering dogs. One of the slaves rescues him by calling off the dogs. Then he is called to the house by a woman who mistakes him for her nephew, coming for a visit. He lets her think he is her nephew—she is supposed to be his Aunt Sally—and makes up a story about his steamboat trip down river to her place. When the woman's husband comes home, she hides Huck under the bed until the proper moment. The man is worried because something may have happened to the boy. After teasing her husband for a while, she hauls Huck out from under the bed. Her husband asks, "Who's that?" She replies, "It's *Tom Sawyer!*" Huck almost faints with relief. He knows enough about the Sawyer family to be able to lie without getting caught. When he hears a steamboat whistle, though, he gets nervous. The real Tom Sawyer may turn up and give him away. He has to get to the landing before Tom gets to the plantation. He tells the Phelps family that he wants to go get his luggage from the place he's hidden it.

> **COMMENT:** Elsewhere Mark Twain tells us that Phelps' farm is a fairly good picture of a farm owned by his uncle. Note how Mark Twain's first-hand experience helps him write a vivid and concrete description of the kind of farm he is describing.
>
> The whole chapter here is an introduction to Jim's escape from slavery. Since Huck's luck in landing at Tom's uncle's farm is highly unlikely—improbable—Mark Twain slides over it by emphasizing not Huck's good fortune, but Huck's discomfort while he's trying to find out who he's supposed to be. To do this Twain builds up a great deal of suspense by having Huck forced to lie about his journey without knowing where he was to have come from, or who he was supposed to be.

CHAPTER 33.   THE PITIFUL ENDING OF ROYALTY

Huck is given one of Phelps' wagons, and he heads for town. Halfway there, he meets Tom Sawyer, who thinks Huck is a ghost. After proving he isn't dead and never was, Huck explains his situation to Tom. Tom tells Huck to take the trunk he has in his wagon, and go back to the farm. Tom will arrive a little later, and Huck is to pretend not to know him. Huck tells Tom that he is going to steal Miss Watson's Jim out of slavery, and asks Tom not to tell on him. He is shocked and surprised when Tom offers to help steal Jim. Huck is so excited by this offer from a boy he considers good, that he gets back to the farm too soon. But Phelps is not a suspicious man, and so everything's all right. A little while later Tom arrives, and after making up a long story about being a stranger and telling where he is from, finally kisses Aunt Sally. Since she doesn't know who he really is, she scolds him. Tom then identifies himself as Sid, his half-brother, who is back in St. Petersburg.

After dinner Huck finds out that Jim has already told Silas Phelps about the fraudulence of "The Royal Nonesuch." He and Tom climb out of their bedroom that night and head for town. They want to warn the king and duke. But it's too late. On their way into town they are passed by a procession of people who have tarred and feathered the king and duke, and are riding them out of town on a fence rail. Huck says: "It was a dreadful thing to see. Human beings *can* be awful cruel to one another."

Huck feels guilty, even though he hasn't done anything wrong. He decides that a person's conscience doesn't have any sense. It takes up a lot of room, but doesn't do any good.

COMMENT: In this chapter we see Huck still following his conscience instead of his reason. He does so because he is by now firmly convinced that theory or reason is a poor adviser and that experiences and feelings are more likely to lead a person right. Although the king and duke used him and Jim shamefully, he is sorry to see them mistreated and cruelly punished.

With Tom Sawyer's return to the story we can expect some more "romantic" games, similar to Tom's teasing of his Aunt Sally. Notice how Tom keeps even Huck in the dark about his plans for pretending to be Sid.

It is important to understand the kind of people Sally and Silas Phelps are. Remember that in the last chapter (32) Sally remarked it was lucky no *people* were killed in the steamboat explosion? Even though she is portrayed as a kind-hearted, loving and warm, humane woman, she evidently didn't consider the Negro a person. Remember, too, that Silas is a good man, innocent and religious—even though he plans to sell Jim for the reward money.

CHAPTER 34.   WE CHEER UP JIM

On their way home, Huck and Tom decide that Jim is probably kept in a hut in the back of the farm, because they saw food being taken there, and the slave that took the food down used a key to unlock and lock the hut. Tom tells Huck to think of a plan to steal Jim, but Huck realizes that Tom is going to come up with a plan that has lots of "style." This is just what happens. Tom discards Huck's plan because it is too simple and easy. Tom's plan, Huck says, "was worth fifteen of mine for style, and would make Jim just as free a man as mine would, and maybe get us all killed besides." When they get home, they examine the hut where they think Jim is kept, and then they go to bed. Huck enters the house by the unlocked door; Tom, however, climbs up the lightning rod—after several unsuccessful attempts.

The next morning they get to see Jim by tagging along with the slave that takes the food down. When Jim sees them he sings out, but they act as though they don't know him. By this they let him understand they are going to do something for him.

COMMENT: In this chapter Tom Sawyer takes over. Notice that the slaves—particularly Jim—seem to fade into the background. They become mainly props, minstrel show Negroes. Tom is not concerned with Jim as a person, or as a friend—the way Huck is. He is interested in a make-believe adventure. Huck knows this, although he doesn't quite understand it. He says that Tom's plan would free Jim just as effectively as his would. What he means is that his simple, direct plan would free Jim just as effectively as Tom's complicated, confusing one. Not only that, but his plan would be a lot less dangerous, and require a lot less work.

The reason for this difference between the two plans is that Tom is interested in method, while Huck is interested in results.

CHAPTER 35.   DARK, DEEP-LAID PLANS

Huck and Tom discuss the plans to dig Jim out of the hut he's locked in. They could easily tear the lock off the door, but Tom wants something more exciting. Huck keeps suggesting quick and easy ways of getting Jim loose, but Tom won't hear of it. He says these methods are too "un-regular." Huck must steal a sheet to make a rope ladder (even though there's nothing Jim can possibly climb); he must steal a shirt so Jim can keep a diary in his own blood (even though Jim can't write); he must steal table-knives to dig Jim out with (even though there are picks and shovels nearby).

> **COMMENT:**   Note how Tom uses his wide reading to dredge up the rules for a proper escape. His reading seems to have consisted entirely of the kind of romantic classics—"Baron Trenck," "Casanova," "Bevenuto Chelleeny," "Henri IV"—which Mark Twain satirizes elsewhere. (See *A Connecticut Yankee in King Arthur's Court* and *Life on the Mississippi*, below.) Notice how Tom is willing to pretend that the job takes thirty-seven years, yet is not willing to pretend a saw is a knife. In the next two chapters we will see what happens to this "integrity."

> The contrast between Huck's world and Tom's world is made sharper in the passage dealing with stealing. Note how Huck can't understand why it's so wrong for him to steal a watermelon, while it's all right for him to steal sheets, shirts, knives, and the like.

CHAPTER 36.   TRYING TO HELP JIM

When they think the household is asleep, Huck and Tom climb down the lightning rod, shut themselves in the lean-to next to Jim's hut, and begin digging up the dirt floor next to the wall of Jim's prison. After a long session of digging with the knives, Tom admits that they have to use the picks and shovels, and pretend they're digging with knives. Tom doesn't feel right about it, however. He'd like to use the knives, but his hands are too blistered from using them.

Next day Tom steals a pewter spoon and brass candlestick to make pens out of so that Jim can write a journal in blood. That night they finish the tunnel under the wall, and get into Jim's prison hut. Jim is glad to see them and wants to leave his prison immediately. Tom convinces him that to escape like that would be highly irregular. Jim agrees to go along with Tom's plan, although he doesn't understand such things and how they belong in the white man's world. At any rate, he's comfortable and well looked after, so he'll put up with his imprisonment. Tom tells him that they'll smuggle in equipment (a rope ladder, etc.) by Nat, the slave who feeds Jim, and by Silas and Sally, who visit him to cheer him up and pray with him.

Next morning the boys smuggle a piece of candlestick to Jim by stuffing it into his bread. They go along to see how it works. Huck says: "when Jim bit into it it most mashed all his teeth out; and there warn't ever anything could 'a' worked better. Tom said so himself." While they're standing there, about eleven dogs crawl into the room through the tunnel, which comes out under Jim's bed. Nat thinks he's being witched, so he faints. Tom gets rid of the dogs and locks the lean-to door. He then sets things up for getting the rope ladder to Jim by telling Nat that he and Huck wll get rid of the witches by putting something into a "witch pie."

> **COMMENT:** The emphasis in this chapter is on the contrast between Huck's level-headed realism and Tom's romantic nonsense. Notice that Tom complains about the morality of using picks and shovels. Tom does not mean the same thing by "moral" that Huck does when he says that people are cruel to each other.
>
> Note that Huck, who has had real adventures on the river—boarding the "Walter Scott," the house of death, being involved with the Grangerfords who all get wiped out by the Shepherdsons, and being involved with the king and the duke—doesn't seem to realize that those were real adventures. Instead he enters into the spirit of Tom's make-believe excitement, just as he was completely fooled by the make-believe excitement of the circus (Chaptr 22).
>
> Notice also that Jim is no longer treated as a warm, feeling human being. He is relegated to an inferior position, mainly because the story is no longer about his escape to freedom. Mark Twain has shifted the emphasis away from Jim's escape to freedom, and placed it on the attitudes and points of view of Huck and Tom. These attitudes and these viewpoints are responsible for the cultural sterility and the ignorant inhumanity of the little backwater villages As Mark Twain says in another place, if it weren't for "romantic" literature of the type Tom Sawyer loves, the Civil War might never have happened. This is probably why the wrecked steamboat, the den of thieves, is called the *Walter Scott*.

CHAPTER 37. JIM GETS HIS WITCH PIE

Tom is bent and determined on making Jim's escape follow all the rules he's distilled from his adventure books. He has to send Jim odds and ends of thinks like a rope-ladder baked in a pie, pens made out of candlesticks and spoons, and many other items, all useless to Jim in his present circumstances. The Phelps household is too well run to permit Tom and Huck to steal the spoons and sheets and shirts they need. Finally, in order to overcome the great risk of detection, they steal things and put them back when they are discovered missing. The boys do this over and over again, until Aunt Sally doesn't know what she has or how much of it. On top of this, they so confuse the poor old woman that she doesn't care whether the whole house or any part of it is carried off.

Tom and Huck bake the pie in a brass warming pan of Silas'. They found the pan in the attic amongst the rest of the family "relics." By telling Nat the pie will keep the witches away, they are able to get him to carry it to Jim on the tray with Jim's food. The boy also puts tin plates stolen from the slave quarters on the tray. Jim hides the rope ladder in his bed, and scratches marks on the plates and throws them out the window hole of his hut.

> **COMMENT:** Notice in this chapter how Tom's plans usually get changed a little due to the need for practicality. The plans are always bigger than the reality, in which Tom ends up "pretending" something is done his way, while it is actually done more realistically.

CHAPTER 38.   HERE A CAPTIVE HEART BUSTED

Tom draws up a coat of arms for Jim, part of which makes sense and part of which doesn't. He refuses to explain the arms to Huck. Huck says, "If it didn't suit him to explain a thing to you, he wouldn't do it."

Then Tom says Jim has to carve sorrowful inscriptions on a rock. Since there are no rocks in Jim's hut, Tom and Huck go to get a grindstone. They are almost squashed by it when it topples over as they are rolling it to the hut. So, they get Jim out of the hut and have him help them. When they get the stone in the hut, they chain Jim up again, and have him start carving the inscriptions. Since Jim can't read or write, Tom has to outline the inscriptions on the rock and let Jim follow the lines. Finally Tom decides to bring Jim spiders, rats, and snakes to keep him company. According to the rules, all prisoners must tame and make pets of whatever animal life infests the prison. If none infests it, some must be imported. Also, according to Tom's rules, every prisoner raises flowers in his cell by watering them with his tears. The boys will have to bring Jim a little weed which grows without sunlight. Jim will have to use onions to draw his tears, and he will have to pretend the tears are produced by his "deep sorrow."

COMMENT: The silly escapades in this chapter—including the release of Jim and his re-imprisonment—point up the character of Tom Sawyer and establish the realistic character of Huck by the strong ironic comment. It is obvious that Jim can be freed at any time, and Tom frees him. But Tom pretends that Jim cannot be freed. He makes a game of the "evasion," as he calls it. Jim is a stage prop, like the case-knives, and the weed, and the rats, snakes and spiders. There is confusion over the importance of the *thing* to be done and the *way* it is to be done.

Huck isn't aware that Tom doesn't know what the coat of arms signifies. Compare Tom's coat of arms with the soliloquy the duke teaches the king in Chapter 21. Notice the resemblance in the fact that both the speech and coat of arms are half-remembered, imperfectly understood collections of jargon and cliché. Notice also that Huck is taken in by both just as neatly as he was taken in by the clown in the circus. The fact that Tom can make himself believed in spite of his obvious ignorance and the fact that Huck got involved with the king and duke in spite of their obvious fradulence come close to stating explicitly the central theme of most of Mark Twain's works. This is that the human race will get itself into hot water no matter what rewards are offered for staying out of hot water.

CHAPTER 39.   TOM WRITES 'NONNAMOUS
LETTERS

The boys catch rats and snakes and spiders to take to Jim. The vermin get loose in the house, upsetting Aunt Sally no end. Finally—three weeks later—everything is ready for the "evasion." It must come soon because Silas Phelps has written to the plantation the king told him Jim escaped from. Since the plantation does not exist, he naturally gets no answer. So he decides to advertise Jim in the St. Louis and New Orleans newspapers. Huck wants to free Jim immediately.

In order to make the escape a proper one, Tom insists on writing anonymous letters to the Phelpses, telling them that Jim is going to be stolen by a group of "cutthroats from over in the Indian Territory." Then he dresses Huck in a frock belonging to one of the slave girls and has him sneak around slipping the letters under the door.

The result is that the family is nervous and jumpy, especially Aunt Polly.

COMMENT: Tom is not happy with having Jim escape easily. He writes the letters in order to give the plot away. He does not have Huck deliver the final letter (which tells the day and time of the "robbery"), but delivers it himself for the excitement and adventure involved. The Phelpses have stationed a Negro outside to guard the family. Tom doesn't even notice that the excitement is somewhat toned down since the guard is sleeping soundly enough to allow Tom to slip the note down the back of his neck.

CHAPTER 40.   A MIXED-UP AND SPLENDID RESCUE

On the day preceding the night they set for Jim's escape, Tom and Huck go fishing and check out the raft. They get home late for supper and notice that the whole family is edgy on account of the last letter. Up in their bedroom after supper Tom discovers that Huck forgot to take butter for the lunch they put together to eat after the getaway. He sends Huck down to the cellar to get it. While Huck is getting the butter, Aunt Sally comes down the cellar. He quickly hides the butter (and the bread he was carrying it on) under his hat. But Aunt Sally sees him and makes him go to the "setting-room" to wait till she comes and has a chance to question him about why he's been down there at this hour. When Huck gets to the "setting-room" he finds it full of farmers—fifteen of them—with guns! He concludes that Tom's letters have ruined the escape.

By the time Aunt Sally comes to question him, the butter under his hat has melted and started oozing down the side of his head. Aunt Sally sees the oozing butter and, after panicking because she thinks his brains are leaking out, pulls his hat off. When she realizes it's only butter, she lets him go, saying that if she'd known all along he wanted something to eat she wouldn't have objected to his being in the cellar.

Once he's free of the "setting-room," Huck goes up to bed as he's told. But intead of settling down for the night, he climbs down the lightning-rod, runs to Jim's hut, and tells Tom about the band of armed farmers. Tom, instead of being frightened, is happy. His plan will be "gaudily" successful. Before they can get moving, however, the hut they are in is surrounded by the farmers. They manage to escape, anyway, with Tom pushing Jim first and Huck second. Tom is last to leave. They manage to evade the farmers who by now are chasing them and shooting, and they make their way to the raft.

Huck and Jim discover that Tom has been shot through the leg, but Tom doesn't mind—he's happy; his plan was successful. Huck and Jim, however, are not so happy. Jim decides to risk his freedom in order to get a doctor for Tom. Huck and Jim override Tom's objections. Tom then gives Huck directions about the proper way to bring a doctor. The directions are as unrealistic as the whole plan to rescue Jim. Huck agrees with Tom and leaves after telling Jim to hide in the woods when he sees the doctor coming.

COMMENT: After the escape, the character of Jim comes once more into the foreground. He is no longer the backdrop for Tom Sawyer's silly adventure-game. He is a person in his own right, acting in a way consistent with the pattern of action he established during the voyage with Huck in the earlier chapters of the novel. Not only is he considerate to the point of sacrificing his freedom for the wounded Tom Sawyer, but is a personality strong enough to overcome Tom's objections. No one—at least not Huck or Jim—has been able to rule Tom Sawyer up to this point.

When Jim makes the offer to sacrifice his freedom, and when Huck realizes he means it, he says the best thing of Jim he can think of: "I knowed he was white inside, and I reckoned he'd say what he did say. . . ." Jim's loyalty is the kind of loyalty Huck admires and tries to live up to throughout the story. Jim is Huck's teacher in this respect. For as with the superstition, so with ideas of social justice: Huck does not believe in superstitions he hasn't seen come true. Those he's seen coming true—the rattlesnake-skin, for instance—he believes in. The others—Miss Watson's praying, for instance—he is skeptical of because they didn't *do* anything.

CHAPTER 41. "MUST 'A' BEEN SPERITS"

Huck finds a doctor and sends him out to the raft. The doctor won't go with Huck because he doesn't think the canoe will hold them both. While he's waiting on shore for the doctor to return, Huck falls asleep. It is broad daylight when he awakes. Fearing that the doctor may have gone home, he checks the house but finds that the doctor hasn't been back since he left last night. Before he can get out to the raft to see what the trouble is, he runs into Silas who takes him home afer he explains that he and Tom joined in the hunt but got separated during the night. At home he sees all the family's friends and neighbors sitting around, eating the Phelpses out of hearth and home, talking about the excitement of the night before. (This is where the title of this chapter is taken from. The neighbors actually enter into the spirit of Tom Sawyer's plan, and enjoy it for the kind of plan it was, though they do claim Jim must have been out of his mind to do all that crazy stuff.) No one suspects the boys of helping Jim escape.

When he sees how worried Silas and Sally are, Huck feels ashamed. He is so ashamed that when he promises Sally he won't climb down the lightning rod to go hunt for Tom—who everybody thinks is lost—he doesn't. But he does slide down the rod three times that night to peep in the window of the front room where he sees Sally waiting up for Tom with tears in her eyes.

COMMENT: Huck is a changed person. The lies he tells the doctor are not so convincing as all the rest he's told so far in the novel.

Once he promises Aunt Sally he won't run out on her, he doesn't run out—even though he wants to join his comrades more than anything he's wanted to do so far.

The neighbors' discussion of the events of the night before parallels in a way the description and acting out by the village loafers of the shooting of Boggs in Chapter 21. The reaction to the real adventure in Chapter 21 is the same as the reaction to the bogus adventure in the chapter before this one. Note Huck's attitude toward the assembled neighbors. Does he understand what's going on? Do you think he understands the similarity to the crowd that went to lynch Sherburn?

CHAPTER 42.   WHY THEY DIDN'T HANG JIM

After breakfast the next morning, Silas goes into town to look for Tom, but comes back without him. He remembers, though, to give his wife the letter he got from the post office the day before, when he found Huck. Before Aunt Sally can open the letter, however, she sees the doctor coming, followed by Tom, carried on a mattress, and Jim, chained. Tom is out of his head from the bullet wound. Silas and the doctor take Tom into the house. Huck follows the men to see what they're going to do with Jim. They are going to hang him, until someone remembers that his owner might show up. When he does come, they will have to pay for Jim. They settle for hitting him—"they give him a cuff or two the side of the head"—and cussing him. He is chained tightly this time.

The doctor comes out and tells the men to go easy on Jim because he helped to save Tom's life at the expense of his freedom. Not only that, he says, but Jim was a good and a faithful nurse. The men leave off the cussing.

Next day Tom wakes up in his right mind, and tells Aunt Sally the whole story of how he and Huck "liberated" Jim. When he finds out that Jim is in chains and under guard, he insists that Jim be let loose immediately. It seems Miss Watson died two months ago and set him free in her will. She was sorry she ever considered selling him down river. While he's explaining that he wanted to set Jim free for the adventure of it, his Aunt Polly comes in. She came down from St. Petersburg because Aunt Sally wrote that Tom and Sid had arrived safety. Polly knew that Sid was nowhere near the Phelpses, and so she went down to investigate. She identifies Tom and Huck.

COMMENT: It is interesting to compare this chapter with Chapter 22, where the mob is turned away by Colonel Sherburn. This mob doesn't hang Jim because it might cost them money. There is no question of justice for Jim. The law of economics prevails: if you destroy a man's property, you pay for it. There is no one here to ask what Jim is charged with, let alone anyone qualified to ask whether he's guilty and to what degree. Only the doctor is respected enough to be listened to. He alone tries to make things easier for Jim. But he's not very effective, is he? The men stop cussing. They keep the chains on, however, as though they have extended a great mercy to Jim. Jim is saved only because of practical considerations.

And what is Huck's reaction? Huck reports the goings-on, and is sympathetic to Jim. But he doesn't make the connection between the injustice being done Jim and the responsibility these men have to see that Jim is treated humanely.

The coincidental death of Mrs. Watson and her equally coincidental will have been regarded by some people as a flaw in the novel. This ending is thought to be weak and fortuitous. In modification of this opinion it ought to be noted that this ending does help explain Tom Sawyer's motives. Huck sees now why Tom Sawyer would be acting like a "low-down Abolitionist." Remember: Tom seems to be Huck's hero all through the book. Every time he has an adventure, or does something "gaudy," he wishes Tom were there to see him and approve. Tom is the young boy who will grow up to be the respectable and successful man in his day. We shall see in the next chapter what is going to become of Huck.

The arrival of Aunt Polly is as fortuitous as the announcement of Jim's emancipation. However, she rounds out the story by confirming Tom's report, thereby guaranteeing Jim's freedom, and by identifying Huck, thereby motivating Aunt Sally to try to adopt him in the next chapter.

CHAPTER THE LAST.   NOTHING MORE TO WRITE

Huck asks Tom what he thought they were going to do after they set a free slave free. Tom says he thought they'd continue down the river, then come up again and have a parade in St. Petersburg to honor Jim for escaping from slavery. Considering that St. Petersburg is in slave territory, Huck figures things ended well as they did.

Jim is released from his chains; Tom gives him $40 for being a good prisoner. Jim reminds Huck of the time he said he'd be rich again, and here he is, rich. Then Tom suggests they all buy outfits and set out for the Indian Territory in search of adventures. Huck is agreeable, but says he doesn't have any money; pap's likely got it all from Judge Thatcher by now. Jim tells Huck that pap was the dead man they saw in the floating house.

Now that Tom is almost well, he carries his bullet "around his neck on a watch-guard for a watch, and is always seeing what time it is, and so there ain't nothing more to write about, and I am rotten glad of it, because if I'd 'a' knowed what trouble it was to make a book I wouldn't 'a' tackled it, and ain't a-going to no more. . . ."

THE END

COMMENT: Everything is neatly wound up in this "Chapter the Last." Jim is free; Tom has his bullet to impress people with; and Huck is setting off for the Indian Territory ahead of the others, because Aunt Sally wants to adopt and civilize him, and he's "been there before."

Notice that so far as his social "adjustment" is concerned, Huck is just about where he was in the beginning of the novel: looking for some way to "get out from under" civilization, and to escape its stifling restrictions.

With pap dead, it turns out that Jim has been Huck's closest companion and a kind of alternate father to him. All during the trip, Jim has looked out for Huck and taught him all the things he should learn in growing up. He stood Huck's watches, and he taught Huck the ways of the birds, and he provided the closest thing Huck has to a religion: the superstition that really works. It works well enough to seem to Huck, the narrator, a proper causal force to keep things going along.

ESSAY QUESTIONS AND ANSWERS ON THE ADVENTURES OF HUCKLEBERRY FINN

1.   What is Huck's attitude toward people he disagrees with? What does this tell us about Huck?

Huck says he learned one thing from pap: never disagree with his kind of people. Let him have his own way. You won't learn anything by disagreeing with him; you'll suffer less in the long run by simply letting him go along his own business, no matter how disagreeable it is to you. Huck says the same thing about Miss Watson. While she describes Heaven to him, he keeps thinking he'd "rather go to the other place." But he doesn't tell her, because it would only get her excited and would do no good. He thinks the same thing when he decides not to tell Jim that the king and the duke are frauds.

In general, then, Huck's attitude seems to be that if you let other people alone, they won't come around disturbing your peace and quiet. There doesn't seem to be any percentage in stirring up trouble by getting people all excited. Things won't be changed. An illustration of this is supplied by Dr. Robinson's warning to the Wilks girls that the king and duke are frauds. In spite of this reasonable man's warning, the girls trust the king and duke until the truth becomes painfully obvious to them. They could have spared themselves a great deal of sorrow if they had listened to the voice of reason.

This tells us that Huck enjoys peace and contentment, that he probably has too little of it in his life, and goes to the mighty, sliding river to escape from the harassment of the widow and her sister and the cruelty of his pap.

2.   Does Huck change at all during the course of the novel? In what way?

Yes, Huck becomes more mature, more human, more self-reliant as a result of his experiences and his association with Jim. Huck learns what real friendship means, and he grows to value and cherish his friendship with Jim. In the beginning of the novel he joins Tom in playing a joke on Jim. But towards the end, he cries when Jim is sold to the Phelps family by the king and the duke. The turning point in Huck's relationship with Jim came when Huck humbled himself after he played the game on Jim the night they were separated on the foggy river.

As a result of this friendship, Huck comes to place more trust in his experiences, rather than in what he's been taught. What he learns out of books is too far removed from daily life to be of any use to him.

He points out to Tom Sawyer that he's interested in *results*, not formalities, when it comes to helping Jim escape. This is a change from what he believed when he joined Tom Sawyer's robber gang in the beginning of the book.

3. What use does Mark Twain make of concrete details of description and character portrayal?

Mark Twain depicts life and people realistically by choosing important concrete details that characterize the people or things he is describing. His description of Silas Phelps' farm, for instance, is drawn in great detail, ranging from the dogs that form the spokes of a wheel around Huck to such a small detail as the logs that form steps over the fence. A character is sketched in by Mark Twain by a few deft touches of dialectal comment, and a short speech. The realism of Mark Twain's writing is a result of his eye for detail and his use of detail in description and analysis.

Little things like the decorations of the Grangerford house add up to give the reader an overall impression of the family. By using the family to represent the finest traditions of the pre-Civil War South, Mark Twain adds concreteness to his comment on conditions there.

4. To what extent is THE ADVENTURES OF HUCKLEBERRY FINN a book of social criticism?

By reflecting Mark Twain's attitudes towards the individuals responsible for the injustices and inhumanities done to the poor and helpless, the book contains much that can be called social comment. In its literary form this comment is called satire. That is, its purpose is to make people recognize their own flaws and laugh at them; by laughing at their own follies and faults, people can be made to change their ways.

In a more direct way, *Huck Finn* is a book of social criticism insofar as Mark Twain describes intolerable ignorance and crudity from Huck's point of view, and has Huck comment on the stupidity and cruelty which underlie them. Huck is quick to see the cruelty of tarring and feathering the king and duke, and of chaining Jim in double irons and putting him on a ration of bread and water.

Huck is the vehicle of Twain's comment even in those passages where he does not understand what's going on. He admires the art of Emmeline Grangerford. But from the way Huck describes the drawings, the reader can only smile at Huck's lack of education and deplore the bad taste of the South's finest families.

5. In what way can Jim be said to be a father to Huck?

We first see Jim in a father-role when he teaches Huck about the ways of the birds. Huck doesn't believe Jim at first, but is forced to admit the wisdom of Jim's lore when the rain comes down and forces the heroes to flee to higher ground. Jim exercises power as Huck's protector and defender in this instance. He helps Huck learn something about the nature of the river and the weather, and he aids him in saving his equipment.

In another way Jim is Huck's father. He provides the standards by which Huck can judge the rightness of people's behavior. Huck didn't learn these things from his father; he couldn't subscribe to the Widow's or Miss Watson's religion; he could only learn from Jim. And the way he does this tells us about Huck. Huck believes only what he sees. If he's told a thing, he suspends judgment on it until he sees it come true. This is the case with the rattlesnake-skin, and it is the case with the bird-lore Jim teaches him.

Finally, Jim looks after Huck by taking his watches for him, allowing Huck to sleep longer. His care for Huck's safety and comfort is almost the same as he would expend on his own children.

6.   To what purpose does Mark Twain devote so much space to Tom Sawyer's fraudulent scheme to free Jim?

Mark Twain develops the contrast between Tom and Huck in the final chapters which deal with Tom's scheme to free Jim. The impersonal approach that Tom takes is perhaps the most striking quality of his plan. He does not care, really, whether Jim is uncomfortable or suffering. He wants the escape to be according to the rules. To this end he is willing to steal things from the Phelpses, although he won't let Huck steal a watermelon for his own comfort and pleasure. This single-minded pursuit of glory and "gaudy" effects is the most important characteristic of the king and the duke, who are Tom Sawyer's grown-up counterparts.

The contrast is perhaps better stated by saying that Huck is more interested in freeing Jim than Tom is. Indeed, after he learns that Tom knew Jim was free all the time, Huck comments that he always knew Tom was too good to be a low-down Abolitionist. Tom is interested in the adventure of the thing. Huck in the result of the adventure.

THE ADVENTURES OF TOM SAWYER

The events of TOM SAWYER happen before those of HUCK FINN.
The story of Tom Sawyer deals with the misadventures, really, of several
children in the little Missouri village of St. Petersburg, about thirty years
before the Civil War. The story takes place, that is, sometime during
the 1830's.

As the story opens we get a picture of Tom Sawyer, his half-brother Sid
and his Aunt Polly. Tom is not the "Model Boy" of the village, nor does
he want to be. As a matter of fact, Tom seems to enjoy being in trouble:
he's in it so often. At this point, he winds up having to work all day
Saturday because he took off from school, and didn't get home until
late at night. But Tom doesn't worry over his troubles; he often develops
new interests to tide him over periods when he's being punished and life is
difficult.

As a punishment, Tom has to whitewash the fence, a chore he finds
very distasteful. By pretending the chore is fun, though, Tom persuades
his friends—Ben Rogers, Billy Fisher, Johnny Miller, and all the rest—to
whitewash the fence. Not only that, but by pretending he wants to do all
the work himself, Tom gets the boys to trade him odds-and-ends of
things for the privilege of doing his work. When the job is done, Aunt
Polly rewards him for doing such good work.

Then Tom goes out to play with Joe Harper, his "bosom friend." They
play war for a while, until time to go home. On his way home, Tom
catches his first sight of Becky Thatcher. He falls in love with her,
forgetting his love for Amy Lawrence. He shows off for a while, but
goes home when Becky doesn't come out of the house after she throws
him a flower. When he gets home, he has another encounter with Sid,
who told on him the day before and got him into trouble. Tom and Sid
don't seem to get along too well; Sid seems to be looking for chances
to ingratiate himself with Aunt Polly at Tom's expense. Tom, of course,
gets even with Sid every time he can.

In Sunday School the next day, Tom gets a chance to show off in front
of Becky and her great and famous father, Judge Thatcher. Tom has
traded other boys some of the "riches" he accumulated the day before,
and received Bible tickets from them. These are tickets that are given
out for memorizing verses of the Bible. When anyone has accumulated
tickets that show he's memorized two thousand verses of the Bible, he's
called up to the front of the room and given a prize: a copy of the
Bible. Tom, who doesn't want to bother learning the verses, covets the
Bible because he yearns for the fuss and notoriety of getting up in front
of everybody to receive his prize. By trading wisely, Tom has managed

to be the only one in Sunday School who has enough tickets to qualify for the Bible. The Judge makes a fuss over Tom—which Tom enjoys—and asks him who the first two Apostles were. Tom doesn't know. He guesses David and Goliath. We don't know what happens next; Mark Twain says only: "Let us draw the curtain of Charity over the rest of the scene."

On Monday morning Tom tries to get out of going to school, but Aunt Polly pulls the tooth he complains about, and sends him anyway. He runs into Huckleberry Finn, the son of the village drunkard, who is carrying a dead cat he got a week ago. Tom is intrigued by this treasure and asks what it's good for. Huck replies that it's good to take warts off, providing you go about it right.

By the time Tom gets to school it's very late. In order to get to sit with Becky Thatcher, Tom confesses that he's late because he stopped to talk with Huckleberry Finn. He is severely punished for fraternizing with the worthless Huck, and gets his wish—he must sit with the girls. The only vacant seat is the one next to Becky. He manages to make friends with her, and is so overwhelmed with love that he botches his lessons all day. During the break for lunch, he and Becky stay behind and promise their love to each other. But Tom makes the unforgivable mistake of mentioning his old girl friend. Becky reacts as most women do—she hates him. Eventually Tom reacts as boys do. He tries to make her stop crying by offering her his greatest treasure, the brass knob off an old fireplace andiron. She refuses his gift, but he leaves it behind for her, and he plays hooky for the rest of the day. He wanders about the woods in a melancholy mood for a while, thinking that he will become a pirate. Soon Joe Harper shows up, and the two boys play "Robin Hood."

That night Huck Finn calls for Tom, and they go to the graveyard to have a try at removing warts with the dead cat. They hope to find devils, but instead, they come upon Injun Joe, a "murderin' half-breed." Injun Joe is there with Muff Potter, stealing a corpse under the supervision of young Doctor Robinson. There is an argument about money, and in the ensuing violence, Potter is knocked unconscious, and Injun Joe stabs the doctor with Potter's knife. The boys run away in fear, and do not see Injun Joe put the bloody knife in Potter's hand. When Potter comes to, Joe promises to help him escape and not to tell that he killed the doctor.

Huck and Tom, meanwhile, get to the tannery, where in fear of their lives they write an oath to keep "mum." They sign the oath in blood. Before long they hear a dog howling; the sign is obvious: someone will die. Then a new noise catches their attention. They follow it and come upon Muff Potter snoring. They are sure the dog is howling a warning that Muff will die. The boys separate; Tom goes home. He is unaware, when he climbs in the window, that Sid is awake. The next morning everybody in the house knows that he was out all knight. Aunt Polly only makes him feel worse by not whipping him. When he gets to school, he finds his brass and iron knob in his desk. His heart is heavy with sorrow.

That afternoon the village learns of the murder. Potter's knife is found, and he's convicted by popular opinion before he's even caught. He comes into town and is taken by the sheriff, and accused of the crime by Injun Joe. Tom and Huck almost let out their secret. They don't want to see an innocent man hanged. But because they are afraid of what Injun Joe will do to them if they tell, they restrain themselves.

Tom's conscience bothers him so much he tosses and talks in his sleep, keeping Sid awake. Tom is bothered so much by this trouble that he won't join the other boys in holding inquests on dead cats—a new fad which results from the sensation caused by the inquest on Dr. Robinson. (Sid notes that Tom is acting funny by not taking an interest in these things.) In order to ease his conscience, Tom takes odds and ends of things to Muff in the jail. Nobody's going to do anything to Injun Joe, in spite of his grave-robbing, because everybody in the village is afraid of him.

In addition to this problem, Tom is troubled by the fact that Becky Thatcher is ill and isn't coming to school. He loses interest in everything —piracy, hoops, war, and all—so much so that Aunt Polly is afraid he's sick and begins feeding him all kinds of patent medicines and trying all new "cures" on him. One day Tom feeds some Pain Killer to the cat, and the cat practically tears the room apart in a frenzy. Aunt Polly asks Tom why he did it, and Tom replies that he did it because he felt sorry for the cat who doesn't have an Aunt to torment it with all kinds of medicines and cures. Polly takes him off the medicines and things; this is a great relief to him.

When Becky gets back to school, Tom is overjoyed. He shouts and leaps about, but to no avail. For when he is near her, Becky says to someone else: "Mf! some people think they're mighty smart—always showing off!" Tom decides to lead a life of crime. Feeling sorry for himself, he plays hooky again. He meets Joe Harper again, and they plan to go over to Jackson's Island—about three miles below St. Petersburg—and live as pirates. They take Huck Finn with them when they go over that night. Huck enjoys being out that way. But Tom and Joe can't sleep. Their consciences bother them for running away from home.

The next day the ferryboat comes out, its cannon booming, to drop loaves with quicksilver in them in an attempt to recover the bodies of the boys, whom the villagers believe to be drowned. Joe wants to go home, but Tom ridicules him scornfully. That night Tom goes over to the village, stops at his Aunt's house where Polly, Sid, Mary, and Joe Harper's mother are gathered, talking. He hides where he can overhear the conversation. They are talking about the boys; Aunt Polly thinks highly of Tom—now that he's "gone." The word is that if the boys or their bodies are not recovered by Sunday morning, the funerals will be held that afternoon without the bodies.

Tom sneaks back to the island, getting there just as Joe and Huck are discussing his disappearance. He tells them of his adventures during the night, and goes to sleep. Later on, in order to keep the others from going home, Tom tells them his secret plan. They decide to stick together, since they have the marvelous secret, and can laze around and "smoke and chatter and brag."

There was no joy or comfort in the village, though. Everyone was sorry for the deaths of the boys. Becky Thatcher wished she hadn't given the knob back to Tom. After the Sunday School next day, the bell tolls for the funeral service. As things go along, there is a rustle in the gallery. It's the three boys; they've been hiding in the gallery listening to their own funeral services! The welcome they receive is the most exciting ever. And Tom basks in the glow of attention he is getting. A regular hero, he feels he no longer needs Becky Thatcher. But Becky wants him back. To gain his attention she talks loudly about a picnic she's going to have along about vacation time. But Tom pretends not to notice or care. He starts paying attention to Amy Lawrence. Becky gets revenge by ignoring Tom in favor of some other boy. Tom sees this and gets downhearted. He goes home. As soon as she notices that Tom isn't around any longer, she chases the other boy away. He understands that Becky's been using him to get back at Tom, and he is angry. He decides to get Tom in trouble by spilling ink on Tom's spelling book. Becky happens to pass the schoolroom window at the time, and she sees him. But she decides not to tell Tom because she's still angry with him for the way he behaved when she was talking about her picnic.

While he's at home for lunch, Tom talks with his Aunt Polly about his escapade on Jackson's Island, and about the visit he made to the house that one night. He and Aunt Polly are happy, so happy, in fact, that she kisses him, making him feel good. He is feeling so good that when he gets back to school he apologizes to Becky. But Becky, realizing she has the upper hand now, acts cold toward him.

Before afternoon classes begin, Becky has a chance to sneak into the classroom and take a peek at the book the teacher keeps locked in his desk. While she's there, engrossed in the book—it's an anatomical textbook—Tom comes into the room, surprising her. In her hurry to put the book away, she tears a page. She's sure she'll be whipped in class, and she's horrified at the thought. Tom thinks she's a regular milksop for worrying about a little caning. After all, he's been whipped in class many times and it never bothered him. Although he's sorry for her, he has too many of his own problems to worry about. The teacher discovers Tom's ink-stained spelling book, and punishes him. Tom doesn't think twice about the whipping he gets; it's all in a day's work, and besides he just might have spilled the ink without realizing it.

A little while later, the teacher takes his book out to read for a while. He notices the torn page, and asks each child—beginning with the girls —whether she tore the page. Just as he gets to Becky Thatcher, Tom jumps up and says he tore the page. He takes the whipping Becky would have got, in order to keep her from being embarrassed in front of the class. Becky is grateful, and loves Tom even more than she did before— for his nobility.

Just before vacation time there is "Examination Exercises Night." On this night, students recite little speeches and pieces of verse and the like to an audience composed of the influential members of the village government and parents. The boys of the village get their revenge on the schoolmaster on this night. They snatch his wig off after having the sign-painter's son gild the teacher's bald head while he's napping after dinner the day of the exam.

Tom is still bothered by the secret he shares with Huck concerning Dr. Robinson's murder. He and Huck feel sorry for Potter all the time. For, though Muff Potter's a drunk and a liar, he's never done anything to hurt anybody. The trial begins, and the boys feel even worse. Tom can't stand to see an innocent man hanged. He goes to Potter's lawyer. Finally, after much evidence is given by people who recognize Potter's hand in the deed, the lawyer calls Tom Sawyer to the stand. Tom tells all he knows. Before Injun Joe can be arrested, he crashes his way out of the courtroom and flees.

Tom and Huck live in fear that Injun Joe will come back. Tom is happy only during the day. At night he is lonely and full of fear and misery.

But his spirits aren't completely destroyed. As long as it's vacation time, he feels, he will find some adventure. The best adventure of all, of course, is to dig for treasure. He finds Huck, and the two boys do some digging. They follow the rules set down by some of the novels that Tom's been reading, but they find nothing. Finally they decide to go up to an abandoned ("haunted") house. While they are there, two men come in. The boys drop their tools when they hear the men coming, and run upstairs. From where they hide they can hear and see all that the men say and do. One of the men, familiar to the boys as the "deaf and dumb Spaniard" who has been seen in the village the past couple of days, turns out to be Injun Joe.

The men talk about some "big job" they are planning in the village. The younger man feels that it is unsafe to use this old house as a meeting place any longer. Injun Joe agrees with him, but adds that they will need it only a short time. He tells the other to go back up river until he's looked the village over some more—he's got to stay because he wants revenge. Before the two men split up, they dig out their money and take $30 or $40 apiece. Instead of putting the rest of their money back under the hearth where they had hidden it before, they decide to bury it until they pull off their big job. Then they can come back to the house and get the money as they head for Texas.

While they're digging the hole to bury the money, they come upon a box full of money that some other gang had hidden many years ago. Then Injun Joe notices that the tools they were digging with had been covered with fresh dirt. They decide it is too dangerous to leave any money in the old house. So they will bury it in Injun Joe's den, "Number Two— under the cross." Just before the two men leave, Injun Joe gets very suspicious because of the tools, and decides to search the house. He is on his way upstairs where the boys are, when the rotten stairway collapses and he falls to the floor. He gives up the search because it is getting dark, and he wants to get his things together before setting out for "Number Two."

Tom is very uncomfortable. He's the only person he can think of that Injun Joe might want to wreak revenge on.

But he isn't so uncomfortable he can't be impressed by all the money he saw. He and Huck set out to find "Number Two." Thinking it's probably a room in one of the taverns, they decide to try all the old keys they can get hold of. But they don't need the keys. Tom tries the door and finds it unlocked. When he opens it, he is surprised to see Injun Joe lying on the floor of the room, drunk and asleep. The boys decide to wait until Injun Joe's out of the room before they try to find the box with the money.

Becky Thatcher comes back to town after a trip to another village (her hometown), and sets a date for the picnic. This distracts Tom's attention from the treasure hunt for a time. The Thatchers charter the ferry boat to take the children to Jackson's Island in the company of a few 18-year-old girls and 23-year-old men. Since the party won't be coming back till late, Mrs. Thatcher tells Becky to stay overnight with someone. But Tom talks Becky out of making plans, because he wants to take her to the Widow Douglas's house. He knows the Widow will have ice cream on hand, and she will be generous with it.

The ferry boat takes the party out to the island, where they eat, then set out to explore the island's main attraction: a large cave. Much later, after dark, the party struggles back to the boat, tired and hungry, and the boat shoves off for the village.

Meanwhile, back in the village, Huck—who has been watching "Number Two"—sees two men coming out. He follows them to the Widow Douglas's house. Just outside the gate, Huck hears Injun Joe plotting to dis-figure the Widow because her late husband—the Justice of the Peace—had horsewhipped him and thrown him in jail.

Huck remembers the Widow's kindness to him. He runs to the nearest house in the village, and sends its occupants, the Welshman and his sons, to help her. The next day the village is all full of talk about the excitement at the Widow's house the night before. Then a new subject comes up: Tom Sawyer and Becky Thatcher are missing! The men of the village turn out to search the cave for them. In the meantime Huck gets sick and is delirious with fever at the house of the Welshman, who is good to Huck because he saved the Widow. Since all the doctors are up at the cave searching for Tom and Becky, the Widow comes down to take care of Huck, whose mother is dead, and whose father is the town drunk.

For three days and three nights the villagers search the cave. Except for a hair-ribbon and some markings on the wall, they find no sign of Tom and Becky.

Tom and Becky, meanwhile, are wandering in the darkness of the cave, their last candles being all used up. After sleeping a bit, Tom takes a kite string from his pocket, ties it to a rock, and uses it as a line to follow back to his starting point. He explores some side caves, until at one point he sees a hand holding a candle come around a corner. He shouts joy-fully, thinking he's been found, until he sees the face that belongs to the hand: Injun Joe! Injun Joe runs away, frightened by the unexpected shout. Tom goes back to Becky, too afraid to do any more exploring.

But as time goes on, the hunger he feels makes him a little bit braver, so he starts out again, leaving Becky behind with one end of the string. This time he's luckier. After following two passages to their dead ends, he follows a third until he sees a little speck of daylight. He gropes his way toward it, then sticks his head and shoulders out, and sees the broad Mississippi below him. He goes back for Becky, convinces her he's really found a way out, and gets her out of the cave. They hail a passing boat which takes them to the mainland, and after they've rested, to St. Peters-burg. The town goes wild in the middle of the night.

After a couple of days of resting, Tom is told of Injun Joe's attempt to take revenge on the Widow, and of Huck's illness. A couple of weeks later, he learns that Judge Thatcher has had the big door on the cave sheathed in boiler iron and triple locked. He faints when he hears this news. The Judge brings him to and asks him what's wrong. He blurts out: "Oh Judge, Injun Joe's in the cave!"

When the cave door is unlocked, the search party—with Tom and the Judge at its head—finds Injun Joe dead on the ground. He has starved to death. They bury him at the mouth of the cave, and his grave becomes a popular tourist attraction.

By and by Huck gets to feeling better. Tom takes him to the island, where they enter the cave through the hole Tom escaped through. They find the money Injun Joe had, together with guns and moccasins and a leather belt and rubbish. They take the money back to the village, thinking to bury it for safekeeping. Before they get to the woods with it, they are found by the Welshman, who asks them whether they have bricks or old metal in the wagon. They tell him it's old metal. He thinks they mean junk. He insists that they go with him to the Widow's house. When they get there, they discover that the Widow is having a party in honor of the Welshman and his sons because they saved her life.

The Widow takes the boys upstairs, where she has clean clothes for them, and tells them to wash up and come downstairs when they're ready. Tom's half-brother Sid comes up, and tells the boys that the Welshman wanted them at the party because he was going to surprise everybody by announcing that Huck was the real hero that night. However, Sid continues, it won't be a surprise, not any more, because everyone knows. Tom cuffs him for ruining the Welshman's surprise out of pure meanness. When he and Huck go down, the festivities begin. Pretty soon the Welshman springs his surprise, which is received with polite but artificial astonishment. Then the Widow says that she's going to adopt Huck, and she gives him some money as a reward for saving her. Tom sees his chance. He hauls out the fortune he and Huck found. It is more money than anyone there has ever seen at one time before, although several people there owned property worth much more than that.

Huck is adopted by the Widow. The boys' money is set out at interest. They each get a dollar a day spending money on weekdays, and half-a-dollar on Sundays. This is quite a bit of money for a boy in a small Southern village.

By and by Huck gets tired of civilization, and leaves the Widow's. But Tom gets him to go back by telling him that he is starting a robber gang, and that only respectable people will be allowed in it. Huck promises to go back to the Widow's because he wants to be a robber, and "if I git to be a reg'lar ripper of a robber, and everybody talking 'bout it, I reckon she'll be proud she snaked me in out of the wet."

COMMENT: Mark Twain indicates in the short preface to this book that the story is primarily an adventure tale for youngsters. It is not, therefore, to be read with the searching criticism of an adult. He indicates that adults may get something out of reading *The Adventures of Tom Sawyer*: an understanding of the life of young people in the small, sleepy villages of the South about thirty years before the Civil War. This is the main attraction of the book.

The escapades of Tom Sawyer are no more than the record of the life of a boy in a small town. What does such a boy do for excitement? He makes it up for himself when it isn't already there. He gets a lot of help from the books he's read—books about knights and robbers and famous kings, all of them written from a romantic point of view, all tending to stir up the imagination of an intelligent youngster.

The character of Tom Sawyer is developed pretty much as a model of what we'd consider today to be a "genuine boy." Tom is basically good, but he's by no means the village's "Model." Nor does he want to be, although his conscience does bother him from time to time. He's sure he'll go to hell for playing hooky, and lying. He's not overly good. But then, he's not everly bad. He comforts Muff Potter, and testifies in his favor—even though his life is endangered by the testimony. He stands by Becky in the cave and in the schoolhouse when he takes her whipping. He befriends Huck Finn. He condemns Sid's meanness. On the other hand, there is no denying the fact that he's a show-off. He likes to be the center of attraction. And of course, he feeds "Pain-Killer" to the cat, and he does lie, and he does fight with other boys.

In some respects Tom is the carrier of Mark Twain's satire. He is portrayed as the product of the kind of reading Mark Twain detested most: the romanticized historical novel. Tom's showiness, his love of the "gaudy," his attempts to make a "big splash," result, as Mark Twain states explicitly in another place, in the kind of courageous man who will unthinkingly cause much sorrow and suffering because he won't recognize a lost cause, or won't do things an easy, realistic way. In other words, he won't be moderate. Such a person overly romanticized the days of knight-errantry, without realistically regarding the hardships and the many perils of medieval life. This is Tom's real failing, not hooky-playing. He fails when he has the opportunity to alleviate Aunt Polly's sorrow, but doesn't. Instead, he lets her (and the entire village) suffer a few more days so that he may return in a "gaudy" manner. The grateful village doesn't mind being made a fool of. But Tom's showmanship is essentially selfish. This is the kind of selfishness stemming from ignorance that Mark Twain saw coming from the type of romantic novel that Sir Walter Scott wrote.

The story itself is very properly called the *Adventures of Tom Sawyer*. It is a loosely unified series of escapades that hangs together mainly because the central character is always the same. There are two plots running through the story at all times, and Tom is the most active character in both of them. The first plot is the love of Tom for Becky. The second includes Tom's quest for treasure and the conflict between Tom and "Injun Joe." Both plots are successfully developed because Tom has a romantic nature, derived as noted above, from his reading. There is very little connection between the two plots other than the fact that the central figure is the same in both.

The plots themselves are developed more or less by coincidental occurences: for example, Huck's illness after the attack on the Widow's house is a sudden one which the reader has not been properly prepared for. But the illness is necessary in order to develop the suspense which is needed to carry the treasure hunt along. Huck mumbles incoherently about the package the two men were seen to carry out of "Number Two," and he leads us to think it's the treasure. But by and by we find out it was a package of burglar tools. In the meantime we're wondering what became of the money. Huck can't go looking for it, and Tom's lost in the cave. The finding of the money in the cave is a clever twist, but again, it seems gratuitously worked out. No reason is ever given to lead us to think that Tom had the time or interest to look for Injun Joe's "robber den" while he was lost in the cave. The point is, of course, that the story ends "gaudily," as Tom would say, on a note of high adventure and excitement.

In the main *The Adventures of Tom Sawyer* has no moral. It is different from adventure stories children like Tom Sawyer must have read, because it is realistic, not romantic. Tom Sawyer is what he is and does what he does because Mark Twain lived and grew up watching boys in his village do the same kinds of things. Indeed, Mark Twain himself lived Tom Sawyer's life.

A CONNECTICUT YANKEE IN KING ARTHUR'S COURT

While touring an English castle, Mark Twain meets a man who seems to know a great deal about ancient armor and medieval life. He gets to know the man, who gives him a manuscript that tells a fascinating story. Twain takes the manuscript to his room and begins to read. The story is told in the first person by its hero, the man Twain met in the old castle.

Hank Morgan, the hero, was at one time a foreman in a Connecticut gun factory. He is a smart man, mechanically inclined, and respected by the men under him, because he not only knows his job, but he even can beat any man who back-talks him. One day he meets his match, however. He is knocked out in a fight with one of his men, who lays him out with a steel bar. When he awakens, he finds himself in a meadow. Before he has time to figure out where he is, he is taken prisoner by Sir Kay the Seneschal, one of King Arthur's knights. Hank, the Yankee, doesn't know he's in sixth-century England, so he supposes Sir Kay is a lunatic escaped from an asylum. He humors Sir Kay while he is being taken to Camelot. During the short time he is left alone at Camelot while Sir Kay "reports in" to Arthur, Hank befriends a young page named Amyas le Poulet, or "Clarence" as he calls him.

As Sir Kay's prisoner, the Yankee will be shown around much like a freak would be, until he's thrown into the dungeon to wait for his friends to ransom him, or for Sir Kay to have him executed. Hank learns from Clarence that he is in the year 528. He knows that there was a total eclipse of the sun in that year. So, when Sir Kay decides to have him burned at the stake, and not wait for the ransom, Hank threatens the court that if he's killed on the day set, he will blot out the light from the sun, and all things will rot in the darkness. Merlin the Magician persuades the king to allow Sir Kay to burn Hank anyway. At twelve noon, just as the torches are being touched to the firewood, the moon crosses the sun, blacking it out.

The people become hysterical. Hank offers to return the full light of the sun if he is made administrator of the kingdom. Arthur consents, much to Merlin's chagrin. Hank has made a bad enemy of Merlin, who begins to try to undermine Hank's reputation among the people. To discredit Merlin once and for all, Hank enlists Clarence's aid. First, as administrator, Hank has Merlin arrested for spreading the rumor that the blotting out of the sun was the only magic Hank knew, and it wouldn't work again if he tried it. Then, Hank and Clarence make up a batch of gunpowder. They put it in Merlin's house—a stone tower—and erect a lightning rod with wires leading to the gunpowder. Hank lets it be known that as an illustration of the magical powers which Merlin questioned, he will cause the lightning to destroy Merlin's tower. He gives a date on which he will do this. On the appointed date, Hank brings Merlin up from the dungeon and, in the king's presence and in full view of the crowd, gives him a chance to use his enchantments to keep Hank's magic from working. After Merlin has sweated over his enchantments for a while, Hank sees a thunderhead coming along. He tells Merlin that the time's up, and goes through a little "magic" routine that ends when the lightning strikes the rod and sets off the gunpowder in Merlin's towers. The effect is spectacular. Nothing is left of the building but a hole where it was. Everyone agrees that Hank's magic is stronger than Merlin's and Hank is now secure in his position as administrator. But Hank rebuilds Merlin's tower out of government money, and gives Merlin the job of forecasting weather—an unpopular job in any century.

Now that he is secure in his position as administrator, Hank builds secret schools—Man Factories—reforms the systems of taxation, organizes a patent office, and puts the knights to use by painting advertisements on their armor and using them as walking billboards. Much of his work, like setting up small Protestant denominations and the Man Factories, is done secretly because he is afraid of opposition from the Roman Catholic Church, which he despises because it is an established religion. Hank does not like established religions, not because they may be right or wrong, but simply because they are established. Hank is a nineteenth-century American, and there's no established religion in democratic America, so there shouldn't be one in England. Hank has decided that he will introduce democracy and machinery to England.

Because of his attitude towards the institution of knighthood—which he considers a wasteful misuse of talent and money—Hank soon finds himself challenged to a joust by Sir Sagramore. By this time Hank has been in the Middle Ages for four years and has got his plans off to a good start. He doesn't like the idea of putting everything aside in order to train for this fight, so he is relieved when he learns that the joust will take place after Sir Sagramore returns from his quest for the Holy Grail. The search for the Grail is generally a long one, mainly because nobody is sure exactly what the Grail is, but also because the knights keep getting lost, and search parties have to go out after them. He takes advantage of the time to further the work of installing modern communications systems—the telephone and the telegraph—and of modernizing mining procedures. But King Arthur decides that Hank must go out and meet some adventures before he can fight Sir Sagramore. After all, it is not proper for a common man, Hank, to fight one of the noblest knights in the land without some knightly adventures under his belt. Hank agrees with Arthur, but keeps putting off the day of setting out.

Finally the day comes when he can no longer put off the quest for adventure. King Arthur sends him off with a maiden named Alisande de Carteloise (Hank calls her Sandy) who escaped from a castle where many noble maidens are being held prisoners by three giant brothers.

The Yankee, by now he is called "Sir Boss," is uncomfortable in his suit of armor, and can hardly stand the strain of the journey. He defeats six or seven knights who challenge him on the road. They surrender when they see him breathing smoke out of his helmet. (They've never heard of pipe-smoking.) They think he's a dragon of some sort. When Sandy tells them that he is Sir Boss, they are happy to surrender, and they ride to Camelot to turn themselves in to Clarence, who was left behind to oversee the works begun by Hank.

Hank and Sandy stop at the castle of Morgan le Fay. She is King Arthur's sister, a witch, and Arthur's worst enemy. Boss meets Morgan, and she impresses him as a nice sort of person. He's sure she's been lied about, until he sees her calmly stab a young page who tripped in her presence. She doesn't know who her guests are and is about to have both Boss and Sandy thrown into the dungeon. Sandy saves them by telling Morgan le Fay that she can't throw Sir Boss in any dungeon without getting that whole castle blown into the air. Since Morgan le Fay has heard of Boss's reputation, she gets scared, and releases the two travelers, saying she knew who he was all the time; she only wanted to see him blast a couple of guards into ashes, that was all.

Boss gets a chance to examine her dungeons, though. And, using his authority as Arthur's administrator, he sets most of Morgan's prisoners free, sending some of them to Clarence for training in the "Man Factories."

Boss and Sandy continue their journey. When they reach their destination, the castle where the ladies are being held captive, Boss is surprised to note that it is a pig-pen full of pigs. Sandy sees the pigs as noble ladies; the Boss sees pigs. Obviously, Sandy makes clear, the ladies are enchanted so that Boss won't want to free them. To satisfy Sandy, Boss buys the pigs from the three swineherds who are guarding them, and drives them to the house Sandy points out. After spending a night in the house with the pigs, Boss finds out that Sandy has no home, but chose this house because noble ladies can't be expected to sleep out of doors. The owners of the house aren't around, so Boss gives the pigs to the servants—to Sandy, he's leaving the "ladies" at the manor until their "families" come to take them "home"—and has the servants clean up the rooms the pigs slept in. Now that the quest is done, Boss hopes Sandy will leave him and go home. But that, it appears, is not the way things are done. She won't leave him until he's defeated by a superior knight.

They set out again, and before they go very far meet a group of pilgrims on their way to a shrine in a place called the Valley of Holiness. The group is jovial enough. Boss and Sandy join it, and shortly overtake another group of travelers, this one an unhappy group. They are slaves, chained together and on their way to market. The Boss reflects on the cruel and inhuman treatment of these people and resolves to outlaw slavery when he gets his opportunity to do so.

The journey is interrupted when the group of pilgrims meets one of Sir Boss' agents who is returning from the Valley of Holiness. He greets them with the bad news that the water of the Holy Fountain has ceased flowing. The monks in charge of the shrine have started offering prayers and sacrifices, and have sent for the two greatest magicians in the realm, the Boss and Merlin. The Boss sends the knight off to Camelot with instructions for Clarence to bring some equipment to the Holy Valley.

Once he gets to the Valley, Boss must await Clarence's arrival. While he's waiting, he lets Merlin try to get the waters running. At the same time he inspects the well and discovers that there is much water in it, but that the water is leaking out of a hole in the wall about 95 feet below the surface. The monks think the water has stopped running because somebody took a bath. The Boss takes advantage of this opportunity to clean things up by telling the monks that when he gets the well running it will be by such powerful magic that no one need be afraid the waters will ever stop again. Then, when Merlin finally gives up, Sir Boss has his men fix the leak and start pumping water out of the well. In the spirit of showmanship he sets off a fireworks display as part of the incantations that restore the waters of the well.

After he gets better from the rheumatism he picked up down in the well, he returns to Camelot. He is unhappy because while he was at the Holy Valley, King Arthur visited there and conducted examinations for officer-candidates for the Army. The king insists on the requirement that all officers be nobility of the fourth generation. Boss manages to work out a compromise, however. There will be two regiments. One will be for nobility only, and will be made up entirely of officers. The other will be a regular fighting unit, and will be staffed with officers drawn from the middle and lower classes. The king will have control over the regiment made up of knights and nobility, and Sir Boss will control the other, useful unit.

Since he's planning to modernize and up-date the sixth century, Boss decides he ought to go among the people and learn what their feelings are. He intends to go out disguised as a peasant. When he asks Arthur's permission, the King not only grants it, but, struck with the novelty of the idea, insists on going with him.

During the course of their travels, Sir Boss sees many things in human nature that make people become the willing slaves of oppressive masters. In one incident Hank and the king are chased by a mob of angry townspeople. They are rescued by an Earl who sells them as slaves. Now in captivity they are taken to markets all over the country by their cruel master. He finds them to be unmarketable because their bearing is not that of slaves, but that of independent persons. Everywhere they are taken they note scenes of cruelty, ignorance, and disease. Finally, they get to London, where Sir Boss manages to make his escape. Before he can set the king free, he is involved in a scuffle, and arrested. By the time he is freed and gets back to the slave quarters, it is morning, and the slaves are nowhere in sight. Hank learns that during the night the slave-trader discovered him missing, and began beating the rest of the slaves. They rose up and killed him. When the murder was discovered, the slaves were all—including Arthur—sentenced to be hanged as soon as possible. Boss finds a telegraph office and calls Clarence at Camelot for help; he orders 500 knights commanded by Sir Lancelot. Then he sets out to find the king, and to try to put off the execution until the knights can arrive: the trip from Camelot to London is a long one for a knight on horse-back. Unhappily, Boss is arrested as the slave who caused his master's death by escaping. All the slaves are to be hanged that day—three hours before the knights are due to arrive from Camelot to rescue them. Just as the hangman drops the noose over Arthur's head, the knights and Lancelot appear, three hours early. Instead of sending them down to London on horses, Clarence thoughtfully provided bicycles. What a victory for modern transportation!

Shortly after his rescue, Sir Boss finds an account of his upcoming joust with Sir Sagramore in the young newspaper. It is written like a medieval romance. The fight itself is to be a climax in Sir Boss's attempts to make the whole institution of knighthood look ridiculous. By making the knights laughingstocks, Boss hopes to destroy a caste system he believes is wasteful and cruel.

During the fighting he manages to unseat many knights with his lasso, until Merlin sneaks up and steals it from him. Then he is forced to pro-tect himself with his pistols. A few knights are killed before the rest of them lose their courage, and Boss is left master of the field.

Now that he's defeated the knights, Boss takes over complete control of England, for all practical purposes. He unwraps all his secretly planned and executed improvements: the railroads, schools, telegraphs and tele-phones, stock exchanges, steamships—all the improvements of nine-teenth-century civilization are there, even phonographs and baseball. Things go well for about three years, and Boss is about to overthrow the Catholic Church—which he's despised all through the book because it's the Established Religion—when his baby gets sick. (We learn now that he has married Sandy since he couldn't get her to go home. They have a boy they named "Hello-Central," the old-fashioned—to us—way of calling the telephone operator.)

The doctors tell Boss to take the baby to a better climate. He does. But this turns out to be a trick to get him out of England while the Church destroys his power there. While Boss is gone, the Church uses Queen Guenivere's adultery with Lancelot as an excuse to ban all the modern conveniences, and to lay an interdict on Boss and his men. That is, ac-cording to Boss, no one is allowed to have anything to do with them under pain of the Church's curse. This is a formidable weapon the

Church has, as Boss learns. His knights leave him, as do most of the men he's sent through the "Man Factory." They have lived too long under the old rules to be able to understand what Boss is trying to do. Before Boss gets back, however, the adultery issue has caused the death of Arthur; the kingdom goes to his nephew Mordred, who is also interdicted. Boss learns all of this from Clarence when he manages to sneak back to Camelot. He also learns that Clarence has made excellent plans for a defense against the Church's knights. With 52 young boys who have remained loyal, Boss and Clarence manage to defeat over 30,000 armed knights. They used electrified barbed wire fences, land mines and Gatling Guns (an early type of machine gun), and were sure of victory, until something dreadful happened.

At this point the handwriting of the manuscript is different. The new writer tells us he is Clarence, and that he is completing Boss' work. He recounts how the Boss was wounded by a dying knight to whom he offered comfort. He was taken to the cave that housed the defenders and was looked after by the men until an old woman came along who offered her services as a nurse. The woman turns out to be Merlin in disguise. He casts a spell on the Boss, a spell which will make him sleep for 1300 years and awaken in the nineteenth century, separated from his home and family.

It is early morning when Mark Twain finishes reading the manuscript. He takes it back to the stranger, who is in his room talking in a delirium. He mumbles about Sandy and the days he has spent in the Middle Ages. He seems to have forgotten that he was ever from the nineteenth century. As Mark Twain stands over him, listening, the stranger dies.

> **COMMENT:** This story is best described as Mark Twain's attack on ignorance, cruelty, poverty and their causes. He is especially clear about what the causes are: a rigid system of intellectual control (as reflected by the Catholic Church in the Middle Ages) and an undemocratic system of inherited nobility. His attacks on both these institutions are sharp and vehement. His hero is obsessed with a sense of mission: he will democratize the world by lowering the status of knighthood, thereby making individual worth the key factor that determines a man's position in society.
>
> He will also undermine the Church's control over society by instituting a system of free schools and by secretly establishing a number of small Protestant denominations which will compete with the Church. The competition will force the Church to take a more liberal view of the world, and require it to use its power and wealth to make the world a better place for the mass of people to live in. In trying to modernize the sixth century, Hank Morgan is taking on a project that's doomed to fail. On one level, the project has to fail because historically there were no changes like those Morgan

proposed, at least not till the nineteenth century. On another level, however, the project must fail because Mark Twain himself didn't believe it could work. All through the book we get hints that Twain believed the people of the middle ages to be almost organically incapable of handling modern ideas. Hank comments several times on the very childlike innocence and wide-eyed wonder of the populace. This immaturity is to be dispelled only after thirteen centuries of hard-fought gains, and not overnight, as Morgan intended. The change cannot be sudden, Clarence maintains in the end of the book; a period of social and intellectual evolution is necessary.

It is at the end of the book that we become aware of the tragedy of the reformer. Sudden and total reform is bound to fail. Only the slow, steady march of small reforms coming over a long period of time has much chance of being successful in the long run. And the resulting "loss of innocence" which happens to Morgan, has painful effects. It leaves him bitter, sorrowful and lonely. The reformer is cut off from his world, without hope of ever returning or of ever succeeding in it. Those who die in the fight—like Clarence—preserve at least the hope that someday something will change for the better. This book summarizes Mark Twain's comments on the satirist's work. It explains the bitterness of his later works. Disillusioned and exhausted by a lifetime spent trying to open the world's eyes, Mark Twain took final refuge in the vinegary world of "Captain Stormfield's Visit to Heaven," and the rest of his later works, overly sentimentalized and disillusioned by turn.

The plot of the story is stretched on the fabric of the Arthurian Legend. All the main points of the Arthur story are there: Merlin's influence, Morgan le Fay's enmity, Guenivere's adultery, Mordred's treachery. But there is one very important difference. The details we get of medieval life are not pleasant ones. The world is full of dirt, ignorance and arrogance. *Poverty* and *discomfort* are the lot of the mass of people; *wealth* and *discomfort* are the lot of the privileged few. The glories of knighthood and the thrill of the quest are largely products of the imagination—for example, Sandy's quest for the ladies who turned out to be pigs. Occurrences that are considered to be miracles turn out to be pious frauds. And, oh, what a lot could have been done with a little bit of soap!

There is a big difference between Mark Twain's version of the medieval world and Walter Scott's. Mark Twain's knights are uncomfortable in the iron suits; Walter Scott isn't generally concerned with the point. Twain's knights are liars, ruffians, and bullies, far from honorable; Scott's are the cream of manhood and even the villains are noble in their way. Where Twain's world is full of dirt and realistically portrayed, Scott's is green and shining and covered over with a romantic haze that excludes the details of day-to-day living. Mark Twain seems to be saying: "Take the world of Walter Scott, and subject it to close scrutiny, and you will find a world as full of villainy, cruelty, ignorance, filth, and violence as you will find on the steamboat named *Walter Scott* in THE ADVENTURES OF HUCKLEBERRY FINN."

LIFE ON THE MISSISSIPPI

Mark Twain begins this account of the big river's "personality" with a brief summary of its early history from the discoveries of the Spanish and French explorers, to the early 1800's, the days just before the steamboats began to be used. He tells us that the river is never the same. Nearly the whole of the river the explorer La Salle traveled on is now dry ground. The "Old Man" changes his course and shifts about with no plan or design.

After the period of initial exploration and settlement, comes a period of commercial exploitation. In the early days, the river was used by keelboatmen and raftsmen who made their livings transporting goods up and down the river. These were rough men, strong, courageous, and profane; but, mainly, they were honest.

Twain includes a selection from HUCKLEBERRY FINN in Chapter II of LIFE ON THE MISSISSIPPI. This material, Twain tells us, comes from a book he has started but not finished.

> **COMMENT:**   This is a passage that deals with Huck's attempt to find out whether he and Jim have passed Cairo, Illinois. Huck swims out to a raft that is passing by to try to overhear a conversation that might give him a clue to his whereabouts. He is discovered by the raftsmen, but manages to talk himself out of trouble. He never finds out what he wants to know from these men. The passage was not included in the final version of *Huckleberry Finn*. Mark Twain includes it here as an illustration of the kind of person the old raftsman was. Twain likes these big, simple men.

The era of the keelboatman and the raftsman is brought to a close by the coming of the steamboat. The steamboat could travel in weeks the route it took a raft months to cover. From this time on, every schoolboy along the Mississippi had an ambition to be a steamboatman in some capacity. Boys left their villages to become clerks, engineers, captains, mates or pilots. One of the great temptations is the excitement of travel. Any village boy who had been to St. Louis or New Orleans was considered somehow different from all the rest of his friends. He had seen all there was worth seeing in the world.

Another reason the boys wanted to be steamboatmen was, of course, the notoriety—or popularity—showered on them. When a steamboat came to town all eyes were on the rugged men who braved the mighty waters. There was a certain flashiness, or "style," to being a pilot, or a mate, or engineer, or clerk on a steamboat.

This ambition and the popularity that went with success in attaining it were not restricted to white boys. Negroes who worked on the boats as barbers or stokers were also looked up to by their communities.

To satisfy his ambition, Mark Twain takes to the Mississippi as a "cub pilot." He is an apprentice to one of the more famous pilots of the day, Horace Bixby. Bixby took him on after he found out that young Sam Clemens had tried to set out for South America with hardly enough money in his pocket to get home on. Clemens learns in short order that piloting a Mississippi river steamboat isn't all fun and glory. He discovers that pilots work a series of four hour watches; this means he will be getting up very early at times. He discovers also that he must learn by rote memory twelve hundred miles of river from both directions. Not only must he be able to tell where he is in the dark, but he must be prepared to know the river in its multitude of aspects at highwater time and lowwater time. He must develop an eye for clues the river offers as to its condition. He must be able to know the depth of the water at any one point while he is still many miles away from it. He must remember everything the river tells him about itself, and everything anyone else tells him about it. He must love his work, and he must spend his leisure time talking about it and thinking about it.

Above all, he must be able to handle a steamboat, and to do so asleep if necessary. Steamboat piloting is a respected and highly paid trade. But it is not an easy one.

The young Sam Clemens soon learns that he can master the river; he can tell where the shoals and snags and channels are. But he loses something of his appreciation of the natural wonder and beauty of the river. He learns that a pilot's judgment must be quick and cool, and his courage unshakeable. His confidence in his knowledge must be deep, for his knowledge provides the basis for the judgments on which valuable cargoes and human lives depend.

Twain recounts several anecdotes of his "cub" days, and briefly describes the days of riverboat racing on the Mississippi. He discusses the forming of the Pilots' Benevolent Association (a union of steamboat pilots), its early difficulties and its final victory as the independent organization representing the interests of the pilots. It helped the pilots gain a living wage, but it also helped them in their work by providing a channel for information about the state of the river. "Association" pilots were the highest paid, the safest, and the most well-informed pilots on the Mississippi.

This portion of the book ends with a narrative of the explosion of the steamboat *Pennsylvania*, in which Twain's brother Henry, a clerk, was killed.

Roughly twenty-one years after he had to leave the river because the Civil War caused a shut-down of commerce, Twain revisits his old haunts. By this time—the early 1880's—many changes have taken place, not least among them the thinning out of the steamboat fleet and its replacement by the railroads and tugboats. The boats left in service are not only old and few, but they are not as sumptuous as the boats of bygone days. The steamboat traffic has been taken over by large companies with a great deal of capital to invest. In the old days, the steamboats were owned by small companies, sometimes by the captain himself. The large companies regulate their operations more carefully than the small companies of the old days ever did. In addition, they added modern loading techniques and machinery which reduces the time and the cost of handling goods. But they still lose their passenger trade to the railroads, which are more convenient, and their freight trade to the tugboats, which haul freight cheaper.

In spite of this loss of steamboat traffic, the federal government pours money into projects to develop and improve the river's navigational aspects. A reason for this is that the river does provide very cheap transportation when it is used by the tugboats, one of which can pull more freight farther in a week than all the railroads could move in an entire summer.

Another reason for the government's expenditures is that the government is trying to control the erratic course of the river and its periodic flooding. Both the flooding and the changing of course wash out entire farms and move large pieces of land from one state to another.

Twain tells a fanciful anecdote that involves a German immigrant in order to lead up to the fact that entire villages are swept away when the river chooses to change its course.

All the federal money is being spent after the Civil Far, of course. The memories of pilots who saw service in the War provide stories of the difficult days during and after the seige of Vicksburg. The changes brought about in Southern villages and states as a result of the War all tend to show the South emerging as an industrial center. There is a good deal of exploitation of freed slaves and resistance to nineteenth-century progress, however. Twain dislikes the false medieval architecture which plagues progressive cities like New Orleans. He typifies it as a result of Sir Walter Scott's influence. All those romantic novels about chivalry never did anyone any good.

He tells us that he took the pen name "Mark Twain" from a river captain named Isaiah Sellers who first used it in writing articles about the river for newspapers. In his first piece of newspaper writing, Clemens poked fun at the captain's articles. He hurt the old man so badly that the captain never wrote again. Years later, when the captain died, Clemens —by now a full-fledged writer—took the captain's pen name for his own. He has been trying to do justice to the name ever since.

Twain visits his old home town, Hannibal, Missouri, and calls to memory the days of his boyhood. He compares things as they were then to things as they are during his visit. Hannibal is a thriving railroad center with a much higher population than it had in his boyhood. His friends are all grown and are mainly successful family people, although a number of his childhood cronies have died.

After this visit he continues up river to towns that weren't there when he was born. The journey ends back in New York, where it started.

COMMENT: This work is the story of Mark Twain's journey down the Mississippi River during the early 1880's. It is somewhat of an autobiographical travelogue. It tells us a great deal about Mark Twain and his background and attitudes. In addition, it tells us a great deal about the Mississippi River Valley. It is a narrative in which are mixed a great many personal recollections and anecdotes that tell us something about Mark Twain and the Mississippi. Twain's eye for detail, and his basic sympathy with the river's ways and its people show up in this work. The work is full of concrete detail and specific information about the river's changes and the character of the towns and villages that interrupt its shores. Other sides of Mark Twain's talent are discovered to us. His tendency to write social criticism—often colored by his "rationalistic" bent and his prejudices—is afforded a place to develop here. For example, the venomous references to Sir Walter Scott and other romantic novelists are made wherever some seamy side of Southern life is exposed. Mark Twain has no sympathy for the sentimentalized, phony medieval architecture of Southern cities, or for the senseless admiration of people who are born into the closed society of a "400," or an "upper crust." His respect for individual initiative and for democracy is too great for that. He doesn't respect the "old days" or the "old ways" simply because they are "old." They must prove that they are better than the new ways before they gain his acceptance. (The trouble with this attitude, of course, is that one is often going off after half-baked ideas and fads. Twain himself lost a lot of money this way.)

The second half of the book, beginning with Chapter 22, is the important part so far as our interest in Mark Twain's attitudes is concerned. For it is in this part that Twain studies and reflects on the changes that time and the war have made in the South. He tells us about the good things that are happening—there are schemes to acclimate the Negro to responsible freedom, to raise the standard of living through industrialization, and to harness the mighty river's power.

Twain also tells us what he thinks caused the War, the poor state of the Southern economy, and the social injustices and stupidities he finds in Southern life.

CRITICAL COMMENTARY ON MARK TWAIN

RECENT CRITICISM. Responsible recent criticism has been engaged in studies of Mark Twain's literary craftsmanship. During the past twenty years there has been a revival of interest in works like *Huckleberry Finn*. The novel is studied as a serious work of fiction which portrays from a legitimate point of view the growth and travels of a boy who lived near the Mississippi River. Walter Blair, for example, studied the chronological history of its composition, from the perspective of a critic interested in what was written and how it was done. His work (*Mark Twain and Huck Finn*, Berkeley, 1960) provides answers to many charges of literary bumbling brought against Twain in times past. A great number of long studies and essays focus on Mark Twain's literary techniques and skills. Notable are those of Leo Marx, Delancey Ferguson, Daniel Hoffman, Lewis Leary, E. Hudson Long, Gladys C. Bellamy, Kenneth Lynn, Constance Rourke, Lionel Trilling, Ray B. West, Jr., and Albert Stone. The list cited here is a short one; it is merely representative of the number of students and the variety of their works and special approaches. Whereas early criticism seems to have dealt with the man and not his works, recent scholars have turned their attention to the writings as the proper sphere of literary inquiry, and the only one in which it is possible to draw conclusions with any degree of expert certitude.

SIGNIFICANCE OF THE RIVER. No reader of HUCKLEBERRY FINN can be unaware of the tremendous flow of the Mississippi River. Some critics, notably T. S. Eliot and Lionel Trilling, have gone so far as to see in the River a kind of symbolic deity, a power sufficient to itself. The River "is not ethical or good," Trilling says, but it helps goodness grow in those people who make it an important element in their lives. It is from this general idea that Trilling develops the theory that Huck is a servant of the River god.

Eliot maintains that the River dominates the structural form of the novel. Both he and Trilling use their conclusions to justify the ending of the novel which has been generally recognized as being weak.

As Leo Marx points out, however, what truth there is in these critics' conclusions does not exonerate Twain of failing to face the philosophical point of his work. The novel ends weakly because Mark Twain could not turn from his own milieu. He had to free Jim, although Jim's freedom was meaningless in the context of the Phelps incidents. The River is used metaphorically, structurally and thematically. Huck sees the big River gliding by and is suffused with a sense of awe and majestic calm. All the adventures begin and end on the River. Jim's freedom—the central point of the novel—involves a journey down the River. But at the same time the River does not determine Jim's freedom, Miss Watson does. And she represents the unthinking pietism and false values that Huck flees from not once, but twice: once when he leaves the Widow's house, and once again when he "lights out" for the Indian Territory ahead of the rest because the Phelpses want to adopt him.

The essays of Lionel Trilling, T. S. Eliot and Leo Marx are the main sources for study of this problem.

CONTEMPORARY ATTITUDES. It was not always this way, however. In the very early days, when Twain was still very much alive and writing, critics scorned his books, and libraries banned them for their vulgarity and "lack of consequence." Others of his contemporary critics praised him as the soul of American humor. In popular esteem Mark Twain rode high, wide and handsome. He earned a fortune satisfying the tastes of the "great American populace" of the nineteenth and early twentieth centuries, while some segments of the intellectual leadership of the country looked on him with feelings of distaste that amounted almost to revulsion. In the main, Twain was revered, and even after his death his work continued to command the respect of the majority of Americans.

EARLY OPINION. Some years after his death in 1910, however, literary theorizing set in. Critics seemed to be less interested in what he did write than in why he didn't write something else. Whether these theories resulted from a surfeit of Freud or from the wave of "anti-patriotism" that grew up in the twentieth century's disenchanted 'teens, or whether the theories arose from a mixture of these two and more, will probably never be known. At any rate, the major problem confronting students of Mark Twain's writings has come to be known as "Mark Twain's Wound."*

* Lewis Leary, ed., A CASEBOOK ON MARK TWAIN'S WOUND (New York, 1962). I cite this work here because it provides a wide selection of relevant critical texts as well as an introduction by Professor Leary which explains the central problem clearly and puts it into proper perspective.

BROOKS AND DE VOTO. In 1920 the critic Van Wyck Brooks published a volume entitled *The Ordeal of Mark Twain.* The work is based on Brooks' belief that the late-nineteenth and early-twentieth century cultural environment of America was not capable of sustaining artistic minds and helping them to grow and produce. Brooks' theory, simplified, is that the American cultural scene was too crassly materialistic to produce writers of great significance. He believed that important American literary men had to separate themselves from their native surrounding in order to allow their talents full room for development. Men like Henry James left America for other soils and climates more congenial to intellectual and artistic pursuits. Men like Ralph Waldo Emerson continued to live here, but separated themselves in spirit from strictly American ideals. They refused to restrict themselves to the intellectual attitudes narrowly characteristic of their natal lands.

In addition to these cultural drawbacks, Twain suffered from psychological experiences which left their mark on his sensitive personality. Further, Brooks felt that Mark Twain was a gifted writer, a man with a great talent, but a man who, unfortunately, had never allowed himself to develop his talent fully.

Searching Twain's biography, Brooks and his followers concluded that Mark Twain had chosen to gain popularity among the masses as "America's funny man," rather than to develop his skill as a serious writer. Twain's life long pursuit after riches and popularity was based on the not-necessarily-true American belief that wealth plus popularity equal success. That Twain chased riches is evident from the fact that he made much money which he invested in an unusual and striking house, and in business ventures (that often had little chance of success: an indication that Twain was no businessman, what *he* may have thought to the contrary notwithstanding). He rode to riches more than once in his lifetime. Each time he did so by becoming the "darling" of the popular audience. But by trying to appeal to the mass audience, Twain degraded himself so that he was unable to write the "serious literature" he had it in him to write. The fault lies with the society which holds up the demon "wealth" as its badge of success.

Brooks and his followers saw other forces as contributing to the repression of Mark Twain's critical artistic skill. Among these were his wife's censorship and delicate literary prudery, and his friend's (William Dean Howells) insistence that he had a great comic talent. Not least of the stunting forces were Mark Twain's boyhood and young manhood days in Southern and Western backwaters among narrow, crude, and provincial people—including his own family, which unsuccessfully chased the rabbit of success like a pack of crippled hounds.

Writers who sided with Brooks in his comment were men like Waldo Frank, Malcolm Cowley, and Upton Sinclair.

DEFENSE OF TWAIN.   Shortly after the appearance of Brooks' work, however, voices began to be heard in defense of Twain's artistry. These defenders held that far from being corrupted by his surroundings, Twain was helped by them. Mark Twain did not think America was crass and vulgar. Far from it; he considered American democracy and the spirit of free enterprise to be better systems than any the world had ever produced. It is obvious that he would not turn his barbed wit against the institutions he respected most. He did turn it against social institutions that he understood to be not honorable and not good. This is as much as we can expect from any man: that he be true to *his* ideals, whether they correspond to those of his society and age, or not.

Men like Carl Van Doren, Henry Seidel Canby, William Lyon Phelps, and Stephen Leacock took issue with Brooks' work. Their criticism ranged from Van Doren's remarks that Brooks had tried to psychoanalyze Twain and had failed, to Leacock's basic attitude that the West made Twain an artist, with the implication that without the West Twain would have been no artist.

Not until 1932, however, did anyone undertake a full scale frontal attack on Brooks' position. In that year, Bernard De Voto, in a book called *Mark Twain's America,* took the position that Twain was a writer of a specific kind of humor: the kind that was found in the works of Petroleum V. Nasby and Artemus Ward, the boisterous local humor of the American West. The loudness and brashness of Twain's work is due to the attitude of the Western frontiersman who not only loved the world and all that he saw in it, but also saw through to the realities of things with eyes uncluttered by the confusing forms that closed up the eyes of more pretentious Eastern writers.

The critical battle lines were drawn between critics who saw Twain as a successful—if superficial—humorist, and those who saw him as a tragic figure ironically hamstrung by the society whose adulation he craved and won.

BIBLIOGRAPHY OF CRITICAL COMMENT

Paperback reprints of most of Mark Twain's popular works are easy to come by, and in general include introductions by critics and scholars. The collected edition of most of Twain's writings—with the exception of the works appearing for the first time in our day—was edited in 1922-1925 by Albert Bigelow Paine under the title *The Writings of Mark Twain*. This 37-volume series is in the collections of most libraries.

Biographies range from Paine's *Mark Twain: A Biography*, New York, 1912, which has the advantage of being the "official" biography, and of being published within two years of Twain's death; to Jerry Allen's *The Adventures of Mark Twain*, New York, 1954, a readable narrative of Twain's life, but less scholarly in style and approach than other biographies. DeLancey Ferguson's biography, *Mark Twain: Man and Legend*, New York, 1943, is perhaps the best one around, although some other works—notably *Sam Clemens of Hannibal* by Dixon Wecter, Boston, 1952—give valuable information about specific parts of Twain's life. Wecter's book is rich in information about Twain's childhood in Hannibal. Background information is easily available in a number of works. Chief among these is Bernard DeVoto's study, *Mark Twain's America*, Boston, 1932. Constance Rourke provides background for an understanding of Mark Twain's place in the annals of American humor in *American Humor: A Study of the National Character*, New York, 1931. Good as counter-balance to De Voto's work cited above is Van Wyck Brooks, *The Ordeal of Mark Twain*, New York, 1920, revised 1933. A valuable survey of the critical war between Brooks and De Voto is provided by Lewis Leary in his casebook on *Mark Twain's Wound*, New York, 1962. Leary provides an introduction and survey of the problems, as well as generous selections from the writings of the critics who became involved in the dispute. He provides further bibliography on related subjects, and in his introduction he provides sane comment on the relevance of most of the material he includes. Another work which provides a summary of the dispute, but provides it in less detail, is Hudson Long's *Mark Twain Handbook*, New York, 1957. In addition to a history of the debate, Long provides a short biography of Mark Twain. This work is valuable as a helpful device in getting to learn the chief directions in Mark Twain studies.

Studies of Mark Twain as a literary artist are plentiful. G. C. Bellamy, *Mark Twain as a Literary Artist*, Norman Oklahoma, 1950; Lewis Leary, *Mark Twain*, Minneapolis, 1959; and E. M. Branch, *The Literary Apprenticeship of Mark Twain*, Urbana, Illinois, 1950; are just some of the many studies worth reading.

Specific studies of each of the major works are cited in most of the works referred to above. However, we might mention Lionel Trilling's introduction to the Rinehart edition of the *Adventures of Huckleberry Finn;* the essay is reprinted in Trilling's *The Liberal Imagination,* New York, 1950. Trilling's views and those of T. S. Eliot (in his Introduction to the Chanticleer Press [Crown Publications] edition of *The Adventures of Huckleberry Finn,* New York, 1950) are discussed by Leo Marx in "Mr. Eliot, Mr. Trilling, and *Huckleberry Finn,*" *American Scholar,* XXII (Autumn. 1953), 423-440.

In addition to Lewis Leary's casebook, there are two other volumes which make scholarly and critical writings available to students. One is Arthur Scott's *Mark Twain: Selected Criticism,* Dallas, 1955. The other is Guy Cardwell's *Mark Twain,* a volume of the *Discussions of Literature* series published by D. C. Heath and Company under the general editorship of Joseph H. Summers.

Personal reminiscences of Mark Twain are provided by two works: William Dean Howells' *My Mark Twain,* New York, 1910; and Clara Clemens' *My Father, Mark Twain,* New York, 1931.

NOTES

NOTES

NOTES

MONARCH® NOTES AND STUDY GUIDES

ARE AVAILABLE AT RETAIL STORES EVERYWHERE

In the event your local bookseller cannot provide you with other Monarch titles you want—

ORDER ON THE FORM BELOW:

Complete order form appears on inside front & back covers for your convenience.

Simply send retail price, local sales tax, if any, plus 25¢ to cover mailing & handling.

IBM #	AUTHOR & TITLE (exactly as shown on title listing)	PRICE
	PLUS ADD'L FOR POSTAGE	25¢
	GRAND TOTAL	

MONARCH® PRESS, a division of Simon & Schuster, Inc.
Mail Service Department, 1 West 39th Street, New York, N.Y. 10018

I enclose................................dollars to cover retail price, local sales tax, plus mailing and handling.

Name_____
(Please print)

Address_____

City_____ State_____ Zip_____

Please send check or money order. We cannot be responsible for cash.